OUTCOME MANAGEMENT

Redesigning Your Business Systems To Achieve Your Vision

C. DAN McARTHUR
LARRY WOMACK

QUALITY RESOURCES ®

A Division of The Kraus Organization Limited

902 Broadway, New York, New York 10010

Most Quality Resources books are available at quantity discounts when purchased in bulk. For more information contact:

Special Sales Department
Quality Resources
A Division of The Kraus Organization Limited
902 Broadway
New York, NY 10010
800-247-8519

Printed in the United States of America

97 96 95   10 9 8 7 6 5 4 3 2 1

Quality Resources   This book is also distributed by:
A Division of The Kraus Organization Limited
902 Broadway   AMACOM Books, a division of
New York, NY 10010   American Management Association
800-247-8519   135 West 50th Street
                                                 New York, NY 10020

                                    ∞
The paper used in this publication meets the minimum requirements of the American National Standard for Information Sciences—Permanence of Paper for Printed Library Materials, ANSI Z39.48–1984.

ISBN 0–527–76292–x (Quality Resources)
ISBN 0–8144–0289–5 (AMACOM Books)

Library of Congress Cataloging-in-Publication Data

McArthur, C. Dan.
    Outcome management : redesigning your business systems to achieve your vision / C. Dan McArthur, Larry Womack.
        p. cm.
    ISBN 0–527–76292–x, — ISBN 0–8144–0289–5
    1. Total quality management 2. Leadership. I. Womack, Larry.
II. Title.
HD62.15.M38 1995
658.4'01—dc20   95-5100
                                                                        CIP

TABLE OF CONTENTS

PREFACE

What's This Book About?

"To complain of the age we live in, to murmur at the present possessors of power, to lament the past, to conceive the extravagant hopes of the future are the common dispositions of the greatest part of mankind."

—Edmund Burke

This book is about attitude. It's about leadership. It's about the convergence of vision, work, and accomplishment.

We've been fortunate to have served many successful business leaders of companies varying in size from upward of 100,000 to as few as 10 employees. What these leaders had in common was the ability to paint a clear picture of the future and to rally their associates in the pursuit of that future. Successful business leaders also have the ability to think and act on several levels simultaneously. In this book, we have identified the processes and concepts used by these successful leaders and created models from which the reader can develop his or her own successful leadership style.

Times change faster than do most minds. Many who lead businesses or manage functions are finding it difficult to react to these changes and nearly impossible to anticipate them. The lines that once separated science, the arts, technology, emotions, and commerce are converging. It is no longer wise or possible to separate work from life, or business pursuits from personal pleasures. We live and work in an age of convergence.

In successful businesses the lines that once separated functions like marketing, management, and operations are also merging or being erased. In the 1970s and 1980s the performance of leaders and managers was measured by their ability to control and conserve. Now their performances must be measured by their ability to know as much about the future as about the present.

We've found that successful leaders and managers operate with a vision of the future and from a set of values that includes respect for the business system in which they work and for the colleagues they lead, serve, or share responsibilities with. Most successful leaders are the same persons at work, in play, and in managing the affairs of their personal lives. The age of convergence requires a holistic approach to thinking, planning, and acting. This age of convergence and rapid change requires an understanding that there is no future in the past.

Many of the ideas and methodologies presented here do, however, have a genesis in the past—our experiences. As our philosophy of outcome management evolved, we found it increasingly important not to rely on our past individual and collective accomplishments to legitimize these concepts and methodologies. Though we occasionally turn to the past for examples, we want to encourage a balanced appreciation for experience and history with a focus on the future. We often turn to allegories to strengthen important points, to stimulate the reader's thinking process, and to present our message in a context separate from linear time and circumstance.

What we mean by no future in the past is that the speed with which technology, knowledge, and information change compels business leaders to respond in untried and unproven ways. Success today comes from building visions, models, and outcomes from the future. Success rarely comes from examining past accomplishments or from building replicas of old successes. For example, the popular notion of *benchmarking*—examining and adopting the best practices of others—is potentially very dangerous because it is an examination of an existing process. A company is better off deciding what the desired outcome or ideal system might be like, and then creating a new strategy from the future to achieve it. At best, benchmarking is one data point in an ongoing intelligence gathering process. Few artists ever gain acclaim from copying the old masters. Studying, yes; copying, no.

We have placed great emphasis on modeling from the future. The paradox of our message is that our understanding and appreciation of the future were gained from our experiences.

Let's take the methodology that has recently been identified as reengineering. In the early 1980s, we began to use a two-track approach in the deployment of quality management systems. This very successful process included one track devoted to continuous improvement, the other to ongoing dynamic change. The two-track approach required that the company's leaders adopt a system view of the company, rather than a process or department view. That meant thinking about and acting on several levels at a time. Multilevel thinking was a new concept when we began to use the two-track approach. Multidimensional thinking, however, has now become the key to successfully leading and managing a company of any size. In today's complex and fast-paced business environment, working on one thing at a time no longer produces the desired results. We've included several models to help readers improve their multidimensional thinking abilities.

What we've tried to communicate, is how to think and act on many levels simultaneously. It sounds more difficult than it really is. But it doesn't matter how hard or easy it is to do. To be a successful leader in today's marketplace, you've got to practice multidimensional system thinking and acting.

The United States stands on the shore of the greatest opportunity and challenge it has ever known. The world of commerce is now and forever one. No other country has the brainpower, the resources, the fortitude, or the determination to dominate international commerce. Americans were so successful during the 1960s and 1970s, however, that we stopped doing the one thing that had made us the greatest of all competitors. We stopped dreaming. While the other nations played catch-up by capitalizing on our old dreams, we sat around on our laurels and our fat wallets until the 1980s hit us right between the eyes—awakening us from our stupor and forcing us back to dreaming again. But now business in America is on the move! And our book is written with the expressed purpose of equipping forward-thinking and -acting business leaders with advanced ideas and methods to meet the new challenges before them and to optimize the opportunities to be found in the marketplace of the future. At a time when the lines between work, play, and values are converging, it is important that leaders understand that it is only through a holistic, collaborative approach to work and life in general that we will find peace, joy, and accomplishment. There is no future in the past.

Winston Churchill said, "The empires of the future are the empires of the mind." We say, "Dream before you think, think before you plan, plan before you act." Our book will help leaders get on with their dreams, plans, and actions through a concept we call outcome management.

The death of Dr. W. Edwards Deming signaled the end of an era in management development. The philosophies espoused and taught by Deming changed the way businesses functioned all over the world. And, as with any emerging philosophy, religion, or cause, the focus was first on the founder—the primary source of the new wisdom. But quality-focused management has matured to the point at which gurus aren't all that useful anymore. What leaders need are teachers, interpreters, coaches, and mentors to help them understand the evolving principles of effective management and how to apply them to the particular demands and needs of their businesses.

Outcome management is not to be viewed as an extension of quality management, nor should it be thought of as another management philosophy altogether. Outcome management is a convergence of experience, creativity, technology, and circumstance. We didn't invent it. We just fashioned what needs to be done into a context that people can understand and use, and called it outcome management. Dr. Deming said, "Managers should manage outcomes. Let the people manage themselves."

INTRODUCTION

The Essentials of Successful Management

"If you wish to hit the center of the target, you must aim a little above it; all arrows are subject to the earth's gravity."

—H. Longfellow

FIVE SUCCESS FACTORS

There are five basic factors that affect a business's success—the wants of the customer, the business ecosystem, the company's structure, strategies, and attitude. Customer wants and the business ecosystem (e.g., shifting factors of commerce, economic conditions, and advancing technologies) are not easily influenced. Structure, strategies, and attitude however, can be influenced. The business philosophy we call outcome management is used to create a winning attitude, a strong yet flexible structure, and dynamic strategies for those who apply its principles. Outcome management also suggests that successful companies are those with leaders who can predict the future needs of the customer and changes in the business ecosystem. That which you cannot influence, you must be able to predict.

SECTION I: READY?
BEYOND CONVENTIONAL THINKING

The first section explains why conventional management and marketing approaches are no longer effective, identifies the new key drivers for effective business performance, and outlines how the outcome management philosophy can help build advanced business systems to meet the ever-changing needs of the customer and the company. It also addresses the most essential success factor, attitude—how leaders can use outcome management to create the right attitude for themselves and their associates and how to ensure that everyone has the right attitude toward the methodology used to build effective business systems.

SECTION II: AIM.
THE BASIS OF UNCONVENTIONAL
THINKING

This section addresses how outcome management strengthens the strategies and structure of an effective management system. Strategies include a quality discipline, a knowledge culture, a competitive fitness program, future-based costing and accounting, a commitment to redesigning systems, a technology plan for creating and operating ideal systems, and a strategy for reducing marketing time and increasing management time.

Much is being written about specific tools for elevating business performance. Continuing business success, however, does not come from the use of a single tool or strategy in lieu of the others. In this section, we discuss a number of the popular business tools, like reengineering, time-based management, activity-based costing, and the need for a new quality discipline. We discuss them, however in the context of integration. The true value of these and other management tools comes from using the right tool at the right time in concert with all the other important activities of the company. Business success comes from integrating vision, missions, knowledge, planning, and work and from applying the appropriate tools in harmony and synchronization.

We also address structure—vision, missions, measures, value, factors, actions, and the future. A mission is not to be confused with a vision. A vision is leadership's desired and stated future for the company. A mission is an action required to achieve an aspect of the vision.

This section is primarily focused, however, on multidimensional thinking—what it is, its value, and how to do it.

SECTION III: FIRE!
MOST EXCELLENT FORMULA

In the final section, we revisit the entire company system, this time as a whole and on an advanced level. This section provides the leader with the special knowledge required to achieve high levels of performance, productivity, and profits—how to, in the words of Aristotle, "make excellence a habit, instead of an event."

Outcome management applied to the structure, strategies, and attitude of a company opens opportunities and challenges unavailable from traditional management methods. Outcome management as a methodology of looking to the future for answers provides a marketing advantage without the limits imposed by history.

DEMING'S LAST CONTRIBUTION

In his later years, Dr. Deming presented his concept of profound knowledge:

- Understanding systems.

- Understanding the theory of variation.

- Understanding the theory of knowledge.

- Understanding the psychology of people and what motivates them at work, home, and play.

Deming's profound knowledge concept was in its formative stage of development at the time of his death. He was on the right track, though, and moving toward a more holistic view of his timeless quality message. A language was developing that is more familiar to the CEO than the old manufacturing-centered rhetoric that many leaders found hard to understand and difficult to follow. Even traditional quality professionals are struggling with their engineering-focused images as the concepts of quality-based management move into a new era of knowledge and development. Deming's work in the profound knowledge arena must continue. It's a worthy pursuit as we move into a new age of management concerns.

SECTION I

Ready? Beyond Conventional Thinking

"In this world the passage of time brings increasing order. Order is the law of nature. If time is an arrow, that arrow points to order. The future is pattern, organization, union, intensification; the past randomness, confusion, disintegration, dissipation."

—Albert Einstein

TIME IS AN ARROW

This quotation from Albert Einstein lays the groundwork for outcome management—an archetype process that leaps first to the future for information and inspiration, instead of drawing on past glories for wisdom and direction.

Outcome management is built on Einstein's hypothesis that the future is pattern and the past disorder. It is a management philosophy that uses inductive reasoning—the act of causing—rather than deductive reasoning—reaching a logical conclusion. You first decide what you want the future to be, image or model that future, then thinking backward, establish a process to bring that future into reality.

The future of a company is always in the hands of its leaders. If the leader really wants to hit the moon, everyone

1

will shoot for the moon. If it is not clear what the leader wants to shoot for, many in the company will end up shooting one another. The same is true within functions and within families.

Over the past decade many new companies, and whole countries, have joined in the contest of shooting arrows at the targets of commerce. The arrows themselves have become more expensive and sophisticated, and the targets more elusive. There was a time when merely shooting the arrows of commerce into the air often produced sufficient results for modest business growth. That is no longer so. Targets must be searched out, and preparation for hitting those targets must be more deliberate and focused. Outcome management begins in the future, where the targets reside, and demands that the target be identified before the shooting begins.

Always aim for the future. There is no future in the past or in the present. "The past is randomness, confusion, disintegration, dissipation," said Einstein. Those are not elements of a successful plan. "The future," he said, "is pattern, organization, union, intensification." Now, those are incumbent to success. It is through modeling the whats and hows of an ideal system that a recognizable pattern is formed. Organization means everyone understands the mission and the target. Union or collaboration occurs when the work and behaviors desired by the company's leadership are clearly defined and strongly supported. Intensification is the dedication to purpose that comes from clear goals, spirited leadership, and a value system that rewards honesty, hardwork, and cooperation of the highest order.

Chapter 1 explores the changes in the business ecosystem that created the need for new management strategies—outcome-focused management. Dr. Deming said to always begin with a theory. If what you were attempting to accomplish fails, find another theory to work from. Our theory is based on the following assumptions:

- There has been a shift to a global buyer-driven economy.

- Technology is advancing rapidly.

- Knowledge is readily available.

- Personal worth has been revalued.

Agree with the assumptions presented in chapter 1, and outcome management becomes a natural extension of your own ideas of how to run a successful business.

CHAPTER 1

The Changing Targets
of Commerce

"For I dipped into the future, far as the human eye could see, saw the vision of the world, and all the wonders that would be."

—Alfred, Lord Tennyson

It takes different skills to successfully run a business in the 1990s than it did 30 years ago. During the previous two decades, most businesses, large and small, operated in a seller's market. The demand for products and services was far greater than the supply, the cost of production was low, the customers were not very demanding of quality, and even the tax laws often rewarded business failure over business success. All of these factors combined to give primacy to the producer and to create the seller's market. Many companies succeeded by merely being in business. Perfunctory attention to marketing and selling strategies was often all that was required. The customer bought with little or no arm-twisting. There was plenty of available discretionary income.

In the old days when an entrepreneur came up with a plan to go into the light bulb manufacturing business, his investors would ask, "How many light bulbs can you make?" "One thousand a day." "How much will it cost you to make them?" "Twenty-five cents each." "What will you sell them for?" "One dollar each." "Great, here's the money."

The assumption was that if you could make them you could sell them. And even if you didn't sell them all, the cost of producing them was so low you could still make a profit. The investor of today wants to know how many you can sell and wants to see the proof, up front!

CHANGING ROLE OF LEADERSHIP

The attitude of many CEOs during those seller's decades was basically to preserve, protect, and control the resources of the company; in fact, most CEOs rose to the top because of their financial management capabilities. Risk-taking was minimal and often unnecessary to produce a reasonable profit. The head of the company usually set the course of action based on financial projections, and the measurements of success were passive, based on historical data. "We did x last year. This year, therefore, we should do y."

Leadership meant managing—conserving and controlling. Dust off your old copy of the American Management Association's *Management Handbook* and you'll see what we mean. Only a few years ago, even the most prestigious graduate business schools were teaching the old controlling, financial-focused management style.

The 1970s provided the wake-up call needed by American business leaders. Japanese products, long considered inferior, began slowly and steadily outselling domestically manufactured products. And only the American buyer knew why. In every consumer market the Japanese tackled, their product became superior. This was the catalyst for the return-to-quality movement in America. Dr. Deming had tried his ideas here first. But we were too fat and sassy to listen. So he took those ideas to Japan—a country with no raw materials and few factories left standing, yet replete with people willing to learn and ready to work. It's taken almost two decades for America to catch up with its foreign competitors. Much credit must go to Dr. Deming for the revitalization of commerce in this country and elsewhere. Though many of his theories and concepts were difficult to understand and had their roots in statistics, engineering, and manufacturing, he was able to gain attention of those in the board rooms and redirect business focus to customer service and away from the short-term focus on this quarter's bottom line.

In the 1990s, the pace of business quickened, the economy shifted from supply to demand, consumers became more discriminating and more frugal, and the marketplace as well as competition became global, instead of mostly border-to-border. The marketplace has become almost totally customer- or buyer-driven, and it will remain so. The customer is truly king and is the driver of planning and decision making in successful companies. The marketplace, however, is changing far faster than the processes of decision making in many U.S. companies. This is especially true in some of the larger, more mature companies that made their successes in the old marketplace. The leaders and the cultures of these companies have yet to make the complete shift from just satisfying the needs of the organization to addressing the demands of the customer as well.

Advancing technology is the primary force that's causing the shift to a buyer's marketplace. Technology has changed the way we think, act, communicate, plan, and perform our daily tasks. It has changed the way we serve our customers and make and deliver products. Even the flow of currency has changed. The other major force of change, spurred on by these technological advances, is global competition. Now, whatever happens in a manufacturing company in Bangkok can affect the profit and loss of a small CPA firm in Sheboygan. The ripple effect of a world economy is real. Commerce of any kind has global implications.

The provincial, organization-focused actions that worked in the old marketplace are no longer effective in the world market. The marketplace has changed and so have the tools, techniques, and actions for capturing it.

Leaders who continue to be attached to the old ways have two choices if the companies they lead are to survive: to retire and turn their companies over to the young turks who are ready and willing to look change in the eye, or to get with the tempo of the times and look to the future for new ways of achieving business success. Experience is no longer to be relied upon in planning a company's future.

UNDERSTANDING SYSTEMS

Growing a company from the future requires a basic understanding of systems and models. In the dictionary, a system is defined using words like *interacting, interdependent, assemblage, group, principles, harmony,* and *network.* There are *ecosystems, weapons systems, communication systems, production systems,* and *management systems.* In this book the company is considered to be the primary system (ecosystem) of commercial undertaking and the interconnected activities within that ecosystem are the subsystems of the enterprise.

System thinking is important to the process of creating challenging futures for the company. System thinking means anticipating the diverse effects of contemplated action. System thinking was not as demanding in the seller's marketplace because products and services were typically narrow in scope and subject to fewer vagaries than in today's business environment.

There was a time when management systems, manufacturing systems, and marketing systems within a company were often viewed as connected but not integrated. Each had goals and objectives that were measured by different metrics; sometimes the objectives were in conflict. There were leaders and managers who even took delight in pitting one department against another. It was thought that competition within the company was healthy and a useful management tactic.

ADDING VALUE

System thinking today is more complicated, multidimensional, and considerably more important. Precious resources like time, money, space, people, and technology cannot be wasted on internal competition or political posturing. The system as a whole must get the primary consideration. In outcome management we have established a single measure for the worth of any activity: It must add value for the customer and to the company (system). We view that as a single measure. If an action adds value for the customer and not the company, the action is not useful. This single measure is system thinking in its purest form.

Even an issue as seemingly simple as a meeting should be measured in terms of the value the meeting adds for the customer and the company. If the meeting doesn't add value for the customer and to the company, it should be canceled.

Alliance Corporate Services, Inc. provides real estate management, strategies, and transaction services to Fortune 500 companies. Using a highly complex proprietary software program, Alliance gathers a company's real estate data from as many as 10 different departments. This data includes lease information, property ownership, maintenance costs, and taxes—more than 1,500 line items. The program centralizes information and provides Alliance and its clients with collected knowledge from which to make real estate decisions that capture millions of dollars in hitherto unknown savings.

The client saves money, and Alliance is compensated for the service. Alliance enters the data into a massive data bank and through statistical analysis is able to predict new areas of potential savings for its clients and prospects. The Alliance corporate property information system adds value for the client in the form of cost savings and adds value for Alliance in income and in increasing knowledge of how to advance the savings of current and future clients.

When we assisted Alliance with the redesign of their business process, their stated goal was to create an artificial intelligence system that would continually elevate services to a growing client base and add to Alliance's knowledge of its customers' needs.

NONTRADITIONAL THINKING

Modeling and developing new systems of production, selling, and servicing require a different kind of system thinking than that usually taught in traditional business schools or learned in traditional company settings. The more challenging the endeavor, the greater the need to think about it and act on it at many levels and dimensions simultaneously. Interaction, interrelationships, harmony, networks, and principles (the system words) take on a more holistic meaning.

The Japanese have been at the forefront of trying to make machines that think fuzzily, like people. The idea is to provide brainlike systems to machines that will allow them to learn as they perform. Fuzzy thinking has more to do with sensing than with calculation. For example, the Japanese have designed a washing machine that uses load sensors to measure the size and texture of the wash load and uses light pulsing sensors to measure dirt in the wash water. Every few seconds, fuzzy thinking turns these measures into patterns of water agitation for different lengths of time: the same process with the same results as an Egyptian woman washing her clothes in the River Nile—observing, learning, and adapting the process as she goes.

Whereas the pragmatist says a thing is *A* or *not A*, fuzzy thinking recognizes the ambiguities of all things. *A* can be a fuzzy *A* and still not be *not A*. Everything is a matter of degree. There is perhaps an infinite spectrum of options instead of just two extremes—a difficult concept to grasp for many who lead business.

Bart Kosko, a faculty member of the physics department at the University of California, is a philosopher-scientist who is a leading theorist in the field of fuzzy thinking. He holds up his hand, palm out, and asks his class, "What is this?" "Your hand," they respond. "What is this?" he says, pointing to his wrist. "Your wrist!" they declare. "Will someone please come forward and show me where my hand ends and my wrist begins?" No one volunteers.

THE STICK

The great samurai warrior and teacher Shuzan once held up his bamboo stick to an assembly of his disciples and stated, "Call this a stick and you assert. Call it not a stick and you negate. Now, do not assert or negate, and what would you call it? Speak! Speak! Speak!" One of the disciples came out of the ranks, took the stick away from the master, and breaking it in two, exclaimed, "What is this?"

THINKING WITH FEELINGS

Solutions, answers, and challenges abound. To capture and create the greatest of them requires fuzzy systems thinking—that is, thinking outside the box and outside the past and present, about many things at one time, thinking with your feelings as well as your brain, thinking about what can be, not what is or was.

Systems are dynamic and changing. Note that we use the term *system thinking* and not *systems analysis*. Systems analysis is at best a stimulus for the invention of better systems; it should never be used as a primary source of data for system redesign. There is no future in the past and no ideal system in the present. The ideal system belongs to the future, and the future is only in the mind of one who conceives it.

There is no line between managing a company, creating products and services, and selling them to customers. There is no line between the company and the customer. All of these actions and elements make up the system we call the company. "Management of a system," said Deming, "is action based upon prediction."

MODELS

A representation, a pattern, an emulation, a visualization, an example, an ideal—these are model words. A model is an imagined version of what can be or a replica of what is or what was. Replicas, however, are of little value in the design of successful business systems. For example, the benchmarking craze that entered management theory and practice a few years ago is basically a process of replication—examining an allegedly ideal system and adopting it as your own. In certain circumstances, that might prove to be a useful process. Benchmarking in its extreme, however, is fraught with danger. While you are examining and designing a new system from another's experience, it is quite possible that your competition is looking to the future for a more elegant answer to the same business challenge.

The kind of modeling we're talking about is futuristic in nature—reaching into the patterns, organization, union, and intensification that can be found only in the future and imaging the ideal. Modeling means creating a new system that will exceed the expectations of the customer in a manner that the customer has yet to envision. It means visualizing a system that provides rewards beyond the expectations of the employees, the stockholders, and the board.

Advances in technology have widened the scope of possibilities in innovative systems design. It is now possible to simulate business models, run various emulations, and increase the predictability of success of particular designs. Modeling is a key component in the successful implementation of the outcome management philosophy. Whereas most management systems rely primarily on historical data when creating new models for new systems, outcome management leaps to the future for wisdom, information, and direction, modeling systems that have never existed. The concept of modeling will be used throughout this book as an instrument of clarification and as a method for building ideal systems. The first model we will explore is the company as a system.

BUSINESS AND ORGANIZATION

The system of a company is best explained if it's divided into two interconnected parts—its organization and its business. As with the hand and the wrist, it is difficult to know where one ends and the other begins. We make the distinction through the following definition: The organization is the structure in which work takes place; business is the outcome of work (Figure 1). No matter what business you are in today, you will be in a different business tomorrow. Customer demands will change, economic conditions will change, products and services will change, distribution channels will change, and so on. Many of these changes will be beyond the control of the company. They should not, however, be beyond the anticipation of the company's leadership.

Success results when a company anticipates market changes and then adapts work (the organization) to effectively and efficiently gain the advantages in the changed market. Form must always follow function. The sole purpose of the organization is to provide the optimum situation (form) from which to address the demands (function) of the customer and the profitability (function) of the company. The organization is the form. Business is the function. Systems redesign means reconfiguring the organization to

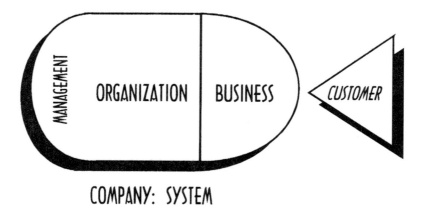

FIGURE 1.   The Company as a System

successfully address the changes that will occur in the marketplace—in the business of the company.

When a company's leaders learn to focus on a desired
outcome (i.e., function) rather than on the processes of creating and delivering products and services (i.e., form), the
concerns over mundane organizational matters and differences disappear.

We received a call from the reservations and sales telemarketing department of a well-known entertainment
company. The woman who headed up the department had
been charged by her superior, a vice-president, to develop
a total quality management (TQM) program. Knowing that
management systems installed in the middle of a company
never work, we attempted to identify the root cause of her
superior's request. We asked why he wanted to implement
TQM at this time. "Employee morale and productivity
problems," she said. We asked what one issue was the
biggest problem in the minds of the telemarketing opera-
tors. "They can't go to the restroom," she replied. "We
never know how many calls are on queue. And," she continued, "our calls are prolonged by having to ask the callers
questions prepared by the marketing department."

"Is the survey information you collect from the callers
useful?" we asked.

"Not to us!" she replied.

The company she works for obviously has a culture more concerned with the processes of its organization than the outcomes of its business. The telemarketing people have no idea how the information they are asked to collect is to be used, and little respect for those asking them to collect it. The attitude is, "They are marketing. We are sales and service. Our business is sales and service. We don't know what their business is, but it's interfering with our work."

Too many companies have cultures that promote this department-oriented view. A focus on perpetuating the organization always creates unhealthy tension between managers and managers, and managers and workers. A focus on the business eliminates barriers and tears down the walls of petty office politics.

THE SYSTEM VIEW

We have identified the elements of the company system as follows: The organization consists of processes, functions, and key systems. Processes are routine activities. Functions are collections of processes. Key systems are the core activities of the company that directly impact business. The business aspect of the system includes the established outcomes and the customer. The organization and the business parts of the system are interconnected through a continuous information loop. That loop also integrates the management system with the other key systems of the company. Figure 2 illustrates these relationships. Outcome management provides a holistic view of the purpose and work of the company as integrated with the demands of the customer.

The company single system model is a way to look at all the plans, work, and results from one perspective and from several dimensions at once. This system model is a theoretical model and continues to grow and change with

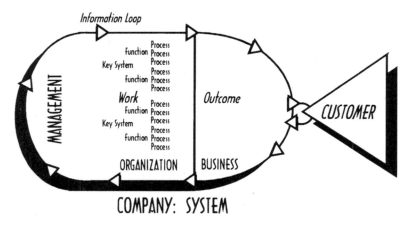

FIGURE 2.   The System View

each examination. The version presented here will differ from the model we will use tomorrow.

MANAGEMENT SYSTEMS

During a brainstorming session we identified 45 allegedly effective management procedures for elevating business performance. These examples, often offered as definitive process archetypes, include total quality management, benchmarking, value creation, core competence, outsourcing, partnering, time-based competition, continuous improvement, operations research, computer-aided "everything," downsizing, rightsizing, the learning organization, core process redesign, and reengineering.

With all these great new paradigms and techniques available to a business leader, it is difficult to realistically identify the concept or concepts that have the highest potential to add value to the company. In many cases workers in companies have become so wary of their leaders and the management paradigm-of-the-week that even the most valuable concepts fail from doubtful and equivocal participation.

From our work and study we have concluded that there are seven essentials to a successful management system. These are not systems within themselves, but the foundation of any successful management system:

- Every company must have a management philosophy that is reflected in the actions and attitudes of its leaders and that is based on a quality discipline.

- Providing knowledge for everyone is a must. Knowledge includes learning and training. People must be trained to do today's job and educated for tomorrow's challenges.

- Every activity must be subject to improvement, integration, elimination, and redesign.

- The cost measures of success must be active, not historical or passive.

- The core competencies (special strengths) of the company must be identified and expanded and driven by market intelligence.

- Time must be viewed as a valued resource. Time reduction in work and time expansion in visioning are the two most important ingredients to success.

- An aggressive information technology strategy is essential. Real-time information and models of ideal systems, collected and manipulated through technology, are the key drivers of successful planning and results.

QUALITY MANAGEMENT'S ROLE

Our roots are in leading and designing successful quality management systems—that is, not the kinds of horror stories told in the business press, but successful systems that produced treasures, often beyond the expectations of the companies and the leaders with whom we worked.

We do not paint with the same strokes as the old masters like Deming, Juran, Feigenbaum, and others, though we have studied and worked with them over the years and pay homage to their contributions to the management art form. Their theories form the foundation of our work and the concepts presented here under the banner of outcome management. Even the term *outcome management* is from Dr. Deming's admonishment to managers: "Manage outcomes. Let the people manage themselves!"

Total quality management is the most misused and misapplied management philosophy ever devised. Ten times more companies have been unsuccessful in deploying TQM than have been successful. In addition, in many successful companies TQM, flow charts, histograms, and process improvement teams are still unknown.

We do believe that the principles on which quality management is based are profound and integral to any successful management system—focus on the customer, work in collaboration (not necessarily in teams), always aim at quality as defined by the customer, and make all work rewarding and purposeful. Indeed these principles will never die.

As the requirements of successful commerce become more complicated and demanding, incremental improvement, the primary goal of TQM, will not be enough to elevate the success of the company. Today's business success requires a more dynamic approach, not at the expense of ongoing incremental improvements, but in addition to them. The principles of quality management still hold true.

Many of the procedures represented here were derived from our work with successful quality management-oriented companies. Some of the processes you will learn about are advancements of ideas developed from these experiences.

Outcome management is an advancement of quality management, particularly in the area of methodology.

Rather than focusing primarily on incremental organizational improvements, however, outcome management focuses on the creation of dynamic business change. Outcome management recognizes that the primary role of leadership is to set the course for the future based on the shifting of customer demands and business needs. In companies with a traditional management system, leaders often relied on others to provide the customer focus for them while they dealt with financially-oriented matters.

Outcome management requires a system view, rather than the process view espoused by most traditional TQM practitioners. System thinking replaces system analysis. And rather than worrying about analyzing, stabilizing, and improving current work, outcome management takes you first to the future for a vision and then back to modeling an ideal system from that future.

TQM is all about process improvement, but why waste time improving something that you may not even need to be doing at all? Outcome management is about effecting dynamic change and incremental improvement at the same time.

CHAPTER 2

Aiming the Arrows of Time—
Leadership

"The probability that the bowman's arrow hits the deer does not lie in the arrow or the deer. It lies in the bowman's mind."

—Bart Kosko

WINNING ATTITUDE

During the first weeks of the 1992–93 NFL season, the Houston Oilers played miserably, losing four out of the first five games. While the sports writers and the fans wanted heads to roll, the team's most important leaders, owner Bud Adams, Coach Jack Pardee, and veteran quarterback Warren Moon, were convinced the problem was one of attitude. They held the course. Houston had built its reputation on the run-and-shoot offense. It was the highest and best use of the team's talent, and change for the sake of change held little or no promise. These three men understood the importance of attitude to winning and of what leadership mettle is all about. They also knew that a winning attitude starts at the top. "Our role," said Coach Jack Pardee, "was to move the players to a new level of excellence by getting them to think more highly of themselves, not by getting them to think more highly of us and our assigned authority." Through the dedication and stay-the-course attitude of its leaders, Houston went on to win nine games in a row and got into the Super Bowl playoffs!

In the first playoff game with Buffalo, however, the Oilers stumbled and reverted to their old ways. The tension on the bench was so high that two of the coaches actually exchanged blows. These were blows to the system from which the team never recovered.

At the beginning of the 1993–94 season, Ray Childress, the awesome Houston defensive tackle, said, "When we won eleven straight last year, we had the best camaraderie I've ever seen—and I've been in football since the fourth grade. I just want to have that feeling again."

When the team was on its winning run, the leaders of the Oilers were engaged in what is called transformational leadership. Many leaders and managers of companies, however, use a transaction style of leadership—the carrot or stick. Carrot-type leaders promise rewards if the work is performed to or above set standards. The stick-type leader—of which there are significantly more—punishes, corrects, or otherwise chastises and threatens the worker when performance falls short.

Transformational leaders, like those at the helm of the 1993 Oilers, act as moral agents, engage in mutual understanding, and celebrate when others in the organization become leaders in their own rights. They lead with conviction and courage. Such leadership is the soul of camaraderie and collaboration.

LEADERSHIP METTLE

One of the major difficulties faced by business leaders is knowing what to let go of and what to hold on to—when to stay the course and when to try something new. Many leaders examine challenges solely from experience and through calculation. Approaching challenging decisions from a purely historical perspective, however, often makes them appear to be insurmountable. When challenges are addressed through calculation alone, the figures often don't add up. Transformational-style leaders, those who lead with vigor, stamina of spirit, and courage, often raise not only the quality of their own performance, but also the performance of those who look to them. In fact, most poor management decisions come about from a lack of mettle or courage, rather than from a lack of information. "Courage," said C.S. Lewis, "is not simply one of the virtues, but the form of every virtue at the testing point." Leadership mettle comes from confidence. Confidence comes from knowing with the mind and with the heart. Leaders with mettle use only one rule for decision making: I'll do it if it feels right. The outcome management environment provides confidence in knowing what is right and strengthens the intuitive decision-making process.

A guiding principle for leaders in an outcome management system is to dream before you think, think before you plan, and plan before you act. It also demands a stamina of spirit, courage of conviction, and leadership mettle.

DREAM, THINK, PLAN, ACT

In a successful outcome management environment, the leader must know as much about the customer as does anyone else in the organization and must truly want to serve that customer in a manner of the highest order. For where the customer is and will be lies the business of the company. If the customer is on the moon, and hitting the moon is the vision, a single individual has to make the final call. That person is the leader.

When business opportunities were boundless, as in the 1950s and 1960s, the value of a clear vision of the future was minimized. In those days the future often arrived on a silver platter with little or no effort from the company or its leaders. Establishing a vision and missions was perceived by many leaders as a meaningless exercise thought up by public relations people for the inside cover of the annual report. Too often a company leader allowed others to craft lofty words about the company and its noble goals, and then signed off on the high-sounding phrases without reflection or interest.

A few years ago we helped an aerospace firm identify and solve a complex cost of quality problem. On our first visit to the company, we joined the quality director in the conference room to discuss the project. There was a maintenance man in the room hanging a plaque with the company's mission statement on it. "Just developed a new mission statement?" we asked. "Yeah," the quality director replied, "the boss had me put one together for the board meeting, and he liked it so well we're hanging it here and in the break rooms around the plant." It is doubtful that the attitude of this CEO or the content of his mission statement will elevate performance, productivity, or profits.

For the sake of clarity, we call the expressions of the future, as articulated by the leader, the vision. Mission in our language means an operation authorized by the senior planning team to develop a new model for a company system.

"WHAT I WANT IS . . ."

The mission statement of that leader at the aerospace company was no vision at all. An effective vision paints a desired picture of how the company will look and perform in time. The leader must draw a vision from an understanding of where the marketplace will be and of what it will take to delight the customer within that future time and space. It must also be based on what the owners of the company want for themselves and their associates within the same time and space. The vision is a prediction of the future of the customer and for the company.

The leader must first conjure a vision, then examine it for challenges and constraints. The most useful way for a leader to express the vision is through a series of clear, simple statements called "*I* wants," not through some well-crafted esoteric statement. Those platitudinal paragraphs written by the public relations department never have really communicated the wishes of the leader to anyone, including the leader. It is easier to follow a list of 20 "I wants," than a vágue four-sentence paragraph.

These "I wants" then become the primary success measures of future missions—not the old historical measures as used in the past but future-positioned targets to aim at and to hit.

Cliff Disbrow is the head of Glaxo Pharmaceutical's Tech/Opts Division in North Carolina. Glaxo is the world's second largest pharmaceutical company. Here are a few of the "I wants" he developed during his visioning process:

- I want us to keep score and post it for our associates to see.

- I want everyone to be given the opportunity to provide input that is listened to and acted upon.

- I want manufacturing costs to remain steady or go lower for the next five years.

- I want us to keep asking why.

The trick in developing a useful set of "I wants" as a vision is to make sure that they are both challenging and achievable. A client who develops separation technology for the solid waste disposal industry told us in an early "I want" development session that he wanted to be "the undisputed leader in his field." We challenged his "I want" by reminding him that there are no footprints in that industry. Because no other company had traveled that path before, education would be his most significant marketing expense. His customers, for the most part, are governments—municipalities in the United States and federal authorities in the European Community and the Far East. These governments must first be educated to the concept of waste separation, then understand the value of it, and if convinced, select a provider through the bidding process.

Being the undisputed leader in that emerging industry would be a costly proposition. He later amended his "I want" to "to maintain the position of being the leading innovator in waste separation technology." His vision now includes selling his company's innovations to other providers of machinery within that industry.

The process of developing a vision for the future is not a secret, exclusive, or haughty process, but it must be a decisive one. If you decide to use this process, take your preliminary thoughts in draft and idea form to your colleagues; allow them to question your desires and elevate your thinking. But give yourself and your colleagues a deadline. The CEO of the waste separator company told his senior staff that he would complete his "I want" vision two months before the annual planning session, to provide them with the measures they would need to develop the specific missions to achieve the vision.

These "I wants" may include projects that will require several years to complete, executive orders ("from this day forth"), and special short-term assignments to be carried out by individuals, alone or in collaboration with others. The "I wants" can be anything you want them to be. That's what leaders are all about. Here's a story of leadership:

VISIONING WITH THE THIRD EYE

A Hindu or Buddhist yogi in tantric meditation experiences an inner bridge in the brain that provides access to what the spiritualists call the "third eye." As the energy rises from the base of his spine, his eyes roll up and he becomes absorbed in the vision seen by the "third eye."

His whole consciousness becomes polarized and at the same time he feels carried up in the vision in an out-of-body experience. He is at once the creator of the vision, a witness to it, and a participant in it.

When one is dreaming of the future, time is condensed. The future seems less foreboding and becomes more easily recognized. Looking at the future with the "third eye" provides a more achievable perspective than viewing it from present or past exploits.

Most successful business leaders began their careers by dreaming. Through intuition they subconsciously followed the ageless process of the yogi in their quest for success—dream before you think, think before you plan, and plan before you act. As their futures overtook them, however, these dreamers became too busy with actions to stay with the process that had brought them to high achievement and they began to shorten the process. Dreaming was the first thing to go, followed soon by thinking. Though they may continue along the path of success, their journeys often become less challenging, less rewarding, and more laborious. It is by rekindling the ability to look at the future from the future that yesterday's dreamers will take the first step toward recapturing the energy, wisdom, and spirit required to meet the exciting challenges of today's more complex and dynamic marketplace. The world has always been shaped by dreamers. Nothing will ever change that.

VISION INTO MISSION

Once leaders have painted a picture of the future and gotten their top people involved in their commitment to it, the senior staff must turn the vision into missions. This process is commonly known as strategic planning. Strategic planning, or any planning for that matter, is no more than developing the most appropriate path for the future and appropriate attitude toward that path. Remember, however, that planning in the 1990s must be business focused, not organization focused. Outcome management means first deciding what business you're in, then adjusting the organization's structure and resources to address the demands of the business. The old way was to look at the organization and its resources, then decide who you wanted the customer to be. That no longer works. To have any meaning at all, planning must begin in the future.

MISSIONS INTO MODELS

Missions are futuristic accomplishments drawn from the vision of leadership. In *Star Trek*, the Federation has a vision of galactic order. From time to time, the Federation calls on Captain Kirk and the crew of the Starship Enterprise to go on a mission to support its vision of galactic order. In a company, the senior staff's role, like that of Captain Kirk and other senior officers of the Federation, is to create and lead missions that will ultimately lead to the future chosen by the leader. To continue with the Star Trek analogy, many of the missions given to the crew are to uncharted and unfamiliar places. Much of what they will need to know to accomplish the mission is unknown to them. Using the ultimate of fuzzy thinking technology, they model potential outcomes and set a course toward the destination and along the path that holds the greatest promise of success.

The role of senior management is to examine the business patterns they hope to find in the future and to build models that appear ideal. The purpose of a major mission (e.g., the redesign of a significant business system) is to create a new system that will exceed the expectations of the customer and increase the value of the company to its owners, leaders, and associates.

Obviously every mission has a different scope, unique parameters, its own significance, and the potential to add a particular increase in value for the customer and the company. During the planning process, the senior staff selects the missions, assigns the work and resources, and establishes the guiding principles.

EXECUTION IS EVERYTHING

The winning coach of the first Super Bowl, Vince Lombardi, said, "Football is blocking and tackling." If the vision and missions are sound and clear, most of the people will know *what* to do (e.g., block and tackle), but they may not know *how* to do it. It's easy to sit on the sidelines and agree with Coach Lombardi. But what if you were handed a helmet, then told that you were the nose guard and to get in there and knock somebody down? Would you know how to do it? To execute and improve work, people need to know not only what to do but how to do it. The role of the leader is to empower everyone in the organization with the skills and knowledge required for them to perform and improve their work. Even to execute fundamentals like blocking and tackling, empowerment is required.

THE ARCHER

The leader is the archer. It is the leader's job to select the targets and arrows, prepare the bow, flex it to its full potential, and let the arrow go. Strategy is the arrow. The organization is the bow. And the targets are the customer's hearts, minds, and pocketbooks.

In outcome management, leaders select the targets of success and articulate them as a vision and missions. Through the wisdom gained from an understanding of the future needs of the customer, the future state of the marketplace, and from co-workers, experts, and business philosophers, the leader flexes the organization and aims it at the selected targets.

The role of leadership is best expressed through a set of clearly articulated precepts—guidelines for learning, planning, and successfully executing the process of leading. Following are the guiding precepts for a leader in an outcome management setting. The precepts are presented here as rules and in a negative framework. As the new order of management begins to unfold, the old order continues to raise points of resistance. We've found that the inexperienced practitioner performs best with rules, hence the admonishing tone of these precepts. Once the new behavior patterns are established, however, the precepts are best embraced from a positive perspective, which is addressed in a later chapter. In addition, some persons find it easier to understand what they must give up to be successful, while others prefer to see what they must take on.

GUIDING PRECEPTS

- **No vagueness:** The primary role of leadership is to provide clear, challenging missions for developing ideal business systems through creation, redesign, or improvement. A mission is best expressed through a direct statement, drawn from the future demands of the customer and the vision from the company's leadership.

- **No tampering:** Processes and systems must be managed. People must be empowered with missions, knowledge, information, tools, and a culture in which they can successfully perform and improve the work. Managers serve their associates by providing consistency and continuity of purpose. Managers establish the attitude and latitude of the worker through a genuine and ongoing empowerment process.

- **No corruption:** Form follows function. The organization's structure, infrastructure, and activities must be driven by the needs of the customer and the business of the company, not by personal needs and ambitions. The organization must always be subject to and ready for change, as must its leaders and managers.

- **No fear:** The leadership must identify and remove all cultural barriers within the organization. It is often easier to succumb to what we fear than it is to attain what we desire. That's why some leaders turn to intimidation as a leadership style. The intimidation style of leadership never produces lofty results.

- **No exceptions:** The system must reward only the desired behavior. If collaboration is the desired behavior, the company's reward system must be based on collaboration.

- **No shortsightedness:** The vision and missions provided by the leadership are the beginning points of planning. What we want is the driver, not what can we make out of what we have.

- **No bias:** The collection of data and information is for enhancing redesign and improvement opportunities. Knowledge is acquired to elevate visioning, planning, and performance, not to verify history or protect personal territory. Training and education must be sequenced to need. Training is provided at the time of the need; education in advance of the need. Both are best learned through experiences, not through lectures.

- **No waste:** The primary application of technology is to model prototype (ideal) systems and to identify improvement opportunities. Technology also

expedites the installation and functioning of redesigns and improvements. The application of technology to work must follow this sequence: identify,
simplify, combine, eliminate, and then automate.
The old hue and cry from the quality movement fits
here: Do it right the first time!

- **No novelty:** The desired outcome drives the selection of redesign and improvement strategies. The
  techniques and tools (strategies) are selected for
  appropriateness, not for novelty (i.e., current management fads). There are many useful methods for
  addressing business challenges. Choose only those
  strategies that provide significant business advantages and that can be positively synthesized with all
  other operative strategies and procedures. Stay
  away from fads and faddish behavior.

- **No insincerity:** Redesign and improvement projects
  must be viewed as a part of work, not as an extra
  layer of labor. There is no line between the routine
  and the special in the valuing of work, only the
  degree of contribution the activity makes to the
  achievement of the vision. Don't organize people to
  make change and then not support them in the
  changes they recommend.

These 10 precepts provide clarity and measure to all
work and serve as the platform of meaningful collaboration.

THE MASTER ARCHER

*In Japan, archery, like many other skills, is distin-
guished as an art. Only a few centuries ago it was a
means of combat; but archery did not fall into disuse with
the advent of modern weaponry. It was cultivated and has
become what we westerners would perceive to be a reli-*

gious ritual. Though no longer a bloody contest, archery is still viewed by its many practitioners as a matter of life and death—a kind of contest of the archers with themselves. The Japanese look inside the archery experience to learn more about their spiritual selves and to learn lessons to apply to their work, health, and personal lives. Archery is taught by master archers. A student describes watching a master archer for the first time:

He nocked an arrow that was over three feet long into the six-foot bamboo bow. He held the bow above his head and in a downward motion drew it so taut that I was afraid it would not stand up to the strain and would lose the arrow. When his left hand, which held the bow, came to eye level with the arm fully outstretched, he remained in this position for a long time before releasing the shot. The arrow whistled by, striking the target some 50 yards away dead center. All of this looked very beautiful and quite effortless. He turned to me and said, "First you must understand the precepts of the art before you become acquainted with the bow. Once I stood where you stand. Once I saw what you saw. Once I held your attitude toward the art. Do not be afraid. Look to the future with courage. One day you will be the master and I the student."

READY? AIM. FIRE!

One of the experiences we often provide our clients at workshops and retreats is an exercise called Ready? Aim. Fire! We set up an archery range with several straw targets, break the group into small teams or imaginary companies, and have them compete with one another. The first round is conducted without any rules. In the second round, each team operates as it desires within certain overall parameters. In the third round, each team competes using identical rules of organizational and overall conduct. The experience advances the concept of collaboration and of how leadership comes from knowledge rather than position. More often than not, those with some knowledge and skill in archery, instead of those higher in the company's pecking order, provide leadership to the process of the exercise.

TRANSFORMATION KEY

Transformational leadership is key to successfully addressing business challenges. Knowing when to stay the course and when to try something new comes from acquiring and using information from the past and present, but more important, from wisdom found only in the future.

Wise leadership comes from having the right attitude, a stamina of spirit, the courage of conviction, knowledge, and from living by the rule: I'll do it if it feels right.

The wise leader provides a clear vision, drawn from an understanding of where the marketplace will be and of what it will take to delight the customer within a future time and space. The vision must also be drawn from what the owners of the company want for themselves and their associates.

The vision serves as the primary measure of business success and as the driver of the missions devised to achieve success. Developing and leading missions are the responsibility of the senior management team. For everyone in the organization to work toward the vision and on the missions, they must be empowered with the proper knowledge, information, tools, and culture.

CHAPTER 3

Drawing the Bow—
Organization

"Leaders have a significant role in creating the state of mind that is society."

—John Gardner

LEADING ORGANIZATIONS

A manager, according to the American Management Association's *Management Handbook,* is one whose power is derived from the position he or she holds and who is accountable for achieving organizational objectives through the actions of subordinates.

Behavioral scientist Bernard T. Bass defines leadership as "the observed effect of one individual's ability to change other people's behaviors by altering their motivations."

Leadership, therefore, is assumed: management is assigned by others or by the system. Both are important to a successful enterprise and are not mutually exclusive.

There is a popular notion being circulated through the latest business books and articles that a manager is the direct opposite of a leader. This notion suggests that managers and leaders sit at opposite ends of a continuum, with leaders at the preferred end.

During the past three decades, however, business in general tilted toward a preference for managers to serve as

CEOs of companies. In the old seller's market, success was often derived through manager behaviors like control, formality, conservation, and analysis. The new notion suggests that managing is no longer effective and must be discarded in favor of leadership.

The outcome management philosophy defies this notion and asserts that success in business requires a balance of leadership and management. The manager is the stone and the leader the fire. Both elements are necessary to forge a successful business venture in the outcome management environment.

LEADER/MANAGER STUDY

In the late 1980s Bass conducted studies to assess the roles of management and leadership in successful organizations. Management is defined as a transactional process—positive and negative reinforcement for performance. Leadership is defined as transformational—inspiring, stimulating, and collaborating toward a vision. The studies indicated that the negative reinforcement style of transactional management (often called the stick approach) usually reduced productivity over the long term. The other side of transactional management—positive reinforcement (the carrot), though contributing to a more pleasant work environment, produced only marginal increases in performance.

The transformational leadership approach was found, however, to significantly raise performance levels and advance job satisfaction as well. Though the results of the Bass study will come as no surprise to business leaders, it is interesting how few decision makers are willing to shift to the more effective transformational style of conducting business.

As the Bass studies indicated, people don't often need or respond well to being managed. They are best led to higher performance. Places, things, and processes, however, are to be managed. Resources must be managed, and tangibles must be controlled.

Occasionally in the life of a growing and changing organization, transactional management is appropriate. A client of ours was having trouble getting one senior staff member to buy into the company's adoption of the quality management business strategy. The senior executive was talking the talk but not walking the walk. "I've tried everything," our client said, "but he's just not getting with the program."

"Are you sure you want this guy on board?" we asked.

"I am," he said. "He could be a valuable member of the team."

Our suggestion to the leader was to call the fellow in, then before he arrived, to hide behind the door. When the fellow came in the leader was to sneak up behind him, grab him by the seat of the pants and the back of the neck, bang the guy's head against the bookshelf, throw him to the floor and put his foot on the senior executive's throat, and say, "Jim, no more fooling around. We are doing outcome management here and you will cooperate or you are out. I don't want your answer now. Either show up Monday morning ready to play with the team or pack your things and get out over the weekend!" Though the leader chose a somewhat less combative action, he did use the stick approach to great advantage and his senior associate has become a valuable member of the team. There are times when the transactional-style of management can be used with positive effect.

But over the long haul people respond best to leadership. Intrinsic intangibles such as brilliant ideas, innovations, and business-altering breakthroughs rarely occur in a tightly-managed environment.

YIN AND YANG

Success in an outcome management environment depends on an appropriate balance of leadership and management (see Figure 3). In business, even leaders must appreciate the value of control, conservation, and analysis, and know when these can be put to effective use. Yet they must balance that appreciation with vision, communication, risk taking, and optimism, particularly in creating an outcome management environment.

As organizations continue to become less structured, the need to inspire performance rather than manage it will increase. As organizations become more virtual or disorganized, people will work more in project collaboration than in departments and layers. They will also be less subject to being managed and routinely directed.

THE DISORGANIZATION

Disorganization is a term coined by Tom Peters in *Liberation Management*. Peters presents a picture of work in a disorganization to be more cerebral and project oriented. In the traditional organized or structured organization, work is more routine and departmentalized—in much the same manner of the old bucket brigade.

Everyone had a place in line and the primary responsibility was to pass the bucket of water up the line until it arrived at the CEO, who sloshed the water on the burning issue and got all the credit for putting out the fire. Advancement meant moving up the brigade to become the dowser or, at the very least, to gain a position where one's deftness with the bucket could be seen by the person in charge. That was the organized organization.

We have come to the edge of the organized organization. Work is now more chaotic and cerebral than laborious. Thinking is the new chore on the shop floor, in the showroom, in the board room, and in the offices of the leaders of the company.

People are working in collaboration instead of in lines, and the customer gets more attention than the quarterly

FIGURE 3.   The Yin and Yang of Business Services

reports. To some the world of business seems out of balance and confusing; to others opportunities abound like never before.

In the organized organization it was possible to move people beyond their competencies into their incompetencies without even noticing it. Longevity, politicking, obedience, and problem solving were the primary performance measures. Leaders rewarded those who put out the fires, whether they were the ones who started them (or let them smolder) or not. In the *disorganization*, people are rewarded based on how well they collaborate.

IT'S NOT JUST TEAMWORK!

If there is a business subject written more about than leadership, it is teamwork. Books and theories abound on how to get people to work in teams. Most problems and opportunities within a company, however, are not best addressed through the work of a team. Many matters are best addressed through a decision by someone in leadership or by someone familiar with the issue—a worker on the shop floor, a clerk in accounting, or a senior marketing vice-president. Other issues are best addressed through the advice and counsel of experts—business consultants, computer gurus, and knowledgeable persons on the company payroll. And yes, some issues are appropriate for the work of a team.

One of the major contributors to the failures of some TQM initiatives was an overemphasis on teamwork. Many companies spent millions of dollars training people to work in teams to solve problems, create new opportunities, and increase productivity. Most of these team-building efforts were eventually abandoned and the quality initiative deemed a failure. Teamwork wasn't the answer. Success comes from people collaborating with one another, not from simply working as a team.

THE LORENZO BROTHERS' CIRCUS

Harrison Caldwell, the manager of the Moog Automotive's Pontotoc Spring Plant in Mississippi, is a client and colleague. When we were visiting Harrison one summer he suggested we attend the circus that was being sponsored by the Pontotoc Lion's Club, of which Harrison is a member. When we arrived at the county fairground we could see the red-and-white striped tent and the ornate sign of the Lorenzo Brothers' Circus.

As we arrived at the ticket table a clown emerged and shouted, "Watch out, here come the elephants!" We stepped aside and watched three stately pachyderms pass to the sounds of the cheering crowd.

The young lady at the ticket table welcomed us and expressed her hope that we'd have a good time. Once inside we were bedazzled by the sights, sounds, and smells. Everything was freshly painted in lively circus colors, the music was exciting, and the smells of food, sawdust, and animals were breathtaking. "Excuse me, gentlemen," said a muscular young man in a sequined cape, "we wouldn't want you to take any unpleasant sou-

venirs home with you." The young man had the largest pooper scooper we'd ever seen. "Just cleaning up behind the elephants," he said moving out the door.

There was no way we could pass the popcorn and cotton candy stand without loading up. The vendor was dressed in a spiffy red jacket with epaulets and gold buttons, and he sported a red bow tie. Just as we took our seats the circus began. The fellow stepped from behind the popcorn wagon, placed his ringmaster's hat on his head, and announced, "Ladies and gentlemen, the Lorenzo Brothers' Circus has begun!" In came the clowns, followed by the ticket taker lady wearing a silver robe with plumes and stars. "I now direct your attention to Marie Lorenzo, the star of the flying trapeze!" Later, one of the clowns was featured as the trainer of the "Performing Pooches" and the gentleman who was cleaning up after the elephants became the bareback rider.

The ushers and confection vendors became costumed elephant riders in the closing parade. Everyone who contributed to the evening's entertainment stood at the exits and thanked each patron for being there.

The next morning on the way to the plant, we drove by the fairground, and just as we expected, there were the trapeze artist, the bareback rider, the clowns, and the ringmaster taking down the tent and packing the gear in preparation for the next performance down the road.

We were never able to identify who, if anyone, was a Lorenzo brother or in charge of the circus. The members of the troop just seemed to assume whatever tasks that needed to be performed at the time. There was no job too large or small to wait for someone else to perform it. Everything that each person did appeared to be focused on delighting the customer and serving the best interest of the circus. Each person was cross-trained, fully empowered, working in collaboration, and driven by the vision and the mission of the Lorenzo Brothers—whoever and wherever they are.

IT'S ATTITUDE

Companies, organizations, sports teams, and families thrive and prosper from an attitude of collaboration. Teamwork is a part of it, but collaboration begins with leadership providing an atmosphere in which collaboration is possible. Collaboration also includes persons working independently, yet toward a common vision. All work in a company is not teamwork.

In preparation for a consulting engagement with the Swiss conglomerate Asea Brown and Boveri, we conducted a study of companies with successful quality management systems. We identified four characteristics that were shared by these companies: Each had what we came to call a family view of the company. The successful companies shared wisdom throughout the organization on an open and regular basis. Each company encouraged, demanded, and rewarded collaboration. And in the top group of these successful companies, we found that work of any and all kinds was integrated at an almost subconscious level.

Family View

A healthy family-type environment in the workplace fosters innovation, creativity, and collaboration. A family view of the company provides traditions, values, common goals, and proper management and distribution of the available resources. Loyalty is implied and never demanded. When good or bad happens, there is instant feedback or corrective action. The family view provides security, assurance, and resources from which individuals can mature and improve their productivity.

Authority and responsibility are fundamental to a healthy functional family of any type. Successful leaders are those who learn how to encourage and stimulate people through the use of transformational behaviors, instead of by transactions (e.g., carrots or sticks) or intimidation. Leadership is most effective when it is established through respect, not through fear.

The successful companies we studied had also developed a common language to ensure that communication was precise and clear.

Shared Wisdom

Once while we were in the conference room of a large printing concern discussing a possible engagement, the company CEO bragged that he had read scores of books on quality management and was well versed on the subject. We asked where he kept those books. He was somewhat puzzled by the question, and stammered that a few were in his office and the others at home. "Why aren't they here in this room, on a shelf, available for everyone to read?" we asked. It was obvious he had never considered the value of sharing the wisdom in those books with his associates and subordinates.

Successful companies have begun to include education as a part of work, instead of as an adjunct to it. Sharing wisdom of all kinds at all levels was a key factor in the success of most of the companies we examined.

The wisdom shared included knowledge and experiences from within the organization, from consulting and coaching relationships, from seminars and workshops, books, tapes, articles, ideas, and market information. The successful companies all had an ongoing wisdom-sharing process.

Collaboration

Collaboration is driven by a shared vision or mission. If everyone knows the target and where it is, and knows that the company's leadership has chosen the target for its value to the overall vision for the company, everyone will work toward it in collaboration.

Psychologists present strong evidence that groups of persons working in concert actually form a group mind that enlarges thought and often leads to a superior collective action. This enlarged or synergistic mind has a tremendous capacity to achieve a potential beyond individual or even group expectations.

The reason for creating projects or missions to be addressed by teams is to take advantage of the value of collaborative thinking. There are managers and workers, however, who find any kind of collective inquiry threatening. That's because most companies preach collaboration and teamwork, yet usually reward individual accomplishments and performances.

Most of the successful companies we looked at had reward systems that were very different from the individual performance reward systems in traditional business systems. They followed the outcome management concept of rewarding collaboration and recognizing individual performance. Each company, however, had a compensation program geared to its own personality, idiosyncracies, and the times.

Reward collaboration, but recognize individual performance. Leaders of companies often wonder why people don't cooperate. The answer is simple: the system doesn't reward cooperation. No single method for rewarding collaboration is appropriate for all situations. Each company must examine its own formal and informal reward systems and build a program to meet its own particular needs.

Collaboration is also a product of the attitude of the company's leadership toward work and the worker. Working as colleagues is the first principle of collaboration.

The second principle is dialogue—continuous communication that includes sharing knowledge and information, providing feedback, and being fully engaged in a mutual quest for clarity and insight.

The third principle of collaboration is open listening. Open listening means suspending prejudices and biases toward the subject and the person speaking. When we learn to think as colleagues, we begin to act as colleagues.

Disagreeing is the fourth principle of collaboration. The real power of seeing another as a colleague comes into play when there are differences of opinion. It is easier to feel collegial when everyone agrees. When there are significant disagreements, it may be a more difficult situation, but the payoff is often much greater. Colleagues celebrate the tension of disagreement and are not threatened by it. Creating the right attitude toward disagreement is a primary responsibility of the company's leadership.

Integrated Actions

The fourth characteristic shared by the successful companies in our study was integrated actions—though not all had achieved the characteristic to the same degree. Integrated action comes from everyone having a system priority. Each individual comes to value the system over the particular process and functions in which they are involved. There is a single measure to determine the value of any activity within an organization. That measure is key to the successful implementation of the outcome management business strategy. Does this activity add value for the customer and to the company? When actions are integrated by this measure, most of the us-versus-them mentality disappears from the company and pride in work becomes a collective pride in accomplishments.

EMPOWERMENT

At Glaxo Pharmaceuticals, senior officer Cliff Disbrow was leading a staff meeting at which he used the word *empowerment*. One of the staff members raised her hand and asked him what he meant by empowerment. He said, "Hell, I don't know! I want everyone in here to write down their definition of empowerment and have it on my desk by Wednesday morning." Pat Carlin, the vice-president of quality, faxed us the 26 definitions and asked us to develop a draft answer for Cliff. At the next staff meeting he defined empowerment as follows: *It's leadership's providing everyone with the knowledge, information, tools, and culture in which they can perform and improve work—in accordance with the company's vision and missions.*

It is the responsibility of the leaders of the company to make sure that everyone has whatever they need to do the jobs that are asked of them.

Empowering Others

Boise Cascade's timber and wood products division provides its senior management team with an operative leadership workshop. The purpose of the activity is to help the attendees understand the power of empowerment and how to use that power. Jim Peterson, the director of quality at Boise, is an energetic fellow who enjoys his work and likes to spread the gospel of quality management. We often invite him to our executive retreats to tell the Boise quality story.

Jim uses the keystone as a symbol for leadership (see Figure 4).

"The keystone," says Jim, "is a wedge-shaped piece at the crown of an arch that locks the other pieces in place. It is also defined in the dictionary as something on which associated things depend for support. The keystone that supports a successful business enterprise is made up of three actions—communicating a vision, establishing trust, and gaining commitment. Those three actions form the keystone of organizational leadership that interlocks and supports all the elements required for business success. Before success comes commitment."

FIGURE 4. The Keystone of Organizational Leadership

"Have you ever seen a successful company that wasn't populated by committed people?" he continues. "Before commitment comes trust. Trust is the emotional glue that binds followers and leaders together. People follow those they trust. Before trust comes a vision. Vision is the most essential element in the keystone of leadership. What is life or work without purpose? Just as the keystone in an arch holds a structure together, the combination of vision, trust, and commitment provides the backbone for organizational character and achievement."

- Vision—The leader must establish a clear vision of the future of the company. The senior staff must establish missions to move the company toward that vision.

- Trust—Trust comes from experience. When deeds match words, trust abounds. When actions do not match words, trust disappears. A leader earns trust. Trust cannot be demanded.

- Commitment—Maintenance and expansion of outcome management require unwavering commitment at the top. As the process progresses, the leaders must be the standard bearers at every step, particularly in the valleys and on the plateaus. If the leader's commitment wavers, he or she can expect everyone to return to the old ways for protection and comfort.

There are three stages of commitment: The first stage is resistance—working actively against the vision or blocking movement toward it through inactivity or delaying tactics. Stage two is invisible resistance—doing what is expected and offering no visible resistance to the vision, but not getting involved in moving it forward. It is often very difficult to identify invisible resistance and to deal with it. The third stage is agreement—partial commitment. Understanding the vision and accepting its worth without being totally convinced that the new way is permanent. Finally commitment is reached—often characterized by enthusiasm, dedication to task, and displays of initiative and creativity.

Invisible resisters are the most difficult to lead. They are usually high up in the organization and see the change in philosophy as a threat to their territory and their value to the company. Often they are right in their fear. These persons are wise enough to be able to hide their true feelings and to develop subtle strategies to undermine the new management initiative. Invisible resisters are sometimes salvageable, sometimes not. As in the earlier case of the resistant executive, dramatic action on the part of the leader is often required to gain true commitment.

Empowering Success

In an effective outcome management environment, employees must be given responsibility for making the entire organization work better, not just for doing their jobs. When teams are formed to address missions or projects, team members must come to the process with a systems view and without concern for departmental issues or self-preservation. Organizations must be flexible and continuously focused on meeting the needs of the customer and the company, not on protecting the current pecking order and maintaining the status quo.

Successful empowerment begins with communicating the vision, establishing trust, and gaining commitment. It moves forward through missions, projects, and assignments drawn from that vision. Empowerment is leadership providing the knowledge, information, tools, and culture with which everyone can perform and improve work—in accordance with the company's vision and missions. Knowledge is the body of intelligence that exists inside and outside the organization and that is needed to make wise and creative decisions. Information is defined as routinely useful data that everyone needs to stay on track, on task, and on vision. Tools are the techniques, processes, and technologies required to perform at peak efficiency. Culture is the context in which work takes place.

Technology has changed the workplace. It is no longer cost-efficient or wise to pass information up and down the management chain. Computers can gather information in an instant, analyze it in a flash, and provide information of such quality that executive decisions are rarely required any more. (No wonder those invisible resisters are afraid!) Smart leaders have always wanted to use wisdom at all levels of the company. But it wasn't until the computer and telecommunications devices made knowledge so readily available that worker-based decisions became viable and cost effective. Glaxo's definition of empowerment was not feasible 10 or 15 years ago. The cost would have been prohibitive and the hierarchical organizational structure wouldn't have allowed it.

If the leaders of a company are responsibly creating a vision developing missions, defining value, and ensuring that everyone has the knowledge, information, tools, and culture with which they can perform and improve work, there is little time to waste on unnecessary tampering with processes and managing the affairs of their associates.

Outcome management focuses the leaders on the future needs of the customer and the company, allowing those responsible for carrying out daily activities to be accountable for them as well.

There are two aspects of a business that need attention every day: the present and the future. If a leader has given everyone else the tools and information they need to address the present, he or she gets more time to focus on the future. Ask yourself, "How much of my time do I spend thinking about and planning the future?" If your answer is "less than 50 percent" something is wrong with your system.

CHAPTER 4

Better Than One—
The Dual-Track Approach

"We have trained them to think of the future as a promised land, which favored heroes attain—not something which everyone reaches at the rate of sixty minutes an hour, whatever he does, whoever he is."

—C.S. Lewis

PROCESS ATTITUDE AND
THE DUAL-TRACK APPROACH

In the previous chapters, we underscored the importance of leadership's establishing and maintaining the proper attitude for success. That includes providing a vision, empowering everyone with whatever they need to be successful in their work, and rewarding appropriate behaviors, which usually means rewarding collaboration. The attitude of the leaders in an outcome management environment must transform people and their work into a cohesive, focused machine by showing stamina of spirit and the courage of conviction and by providing common tools with which to build success. One of the most important tools for leaders to provide is a standardized methodology for addressing challenges. Though all work is not performed in teams, most dynamic challenges for improvement and change do require collaboration. By providing specific missions and common processes for addressing opportunities, leaders ensure maximum value from the work of teams. The basic methodology of outcome management for addressing missions and projects and for working in teams is drawn from the quality management movement. We call it the dual-track approach. Because the process is always led by the senior staff, there should be no question within the organization as to its validity as the project methodology of the company.

The two-track management methodology was first used in the early 1980s as a process to kick off a new quality management initiative. The typical single-track method focused solely on incremental improvements. The prevailing theory was that total quality management was successful only over time and that it required extensive training for everyone in statistical tools and measures. The focus of TQM was on gathering data from the customer and from the system to determine how work might be improved to better address the needs of the customer.

Most consultants and practitioners recommended that organizations start slowly and, as knowledge and experience increased, tackle more challenging problems and opportunities. The belief was that commitment to the new management philosophy would grow with each improvement. Though many companies found the single-track approach useful, other companies abandoned their quality efforts because they found progress to be too slow, the cost of the extensive technical training too high, commitment slow to come, and the effect on the bottom line minimal.

We determined, however, that quality management deployment would be more effective if it followed two tracks simultaneously and that a company is best served if it identifies a single significant project to initiate the process—going with a big bang *instead* of a series of whimpers. By beginning with a big project—one with the potential to significantly improve business—management would send a resounding message that it was serious about the adjustment in its business philosophy and that a big bang project in and of itself could provide sufficient cost savings to self-fund the entire quality initiative. Over time we found that the two-track practitioners outperformed the traditional single-track TQM companies by quantum leaps and bounds. The most difficult task we faced was keeping our clients from abandoning the less dynamic incremental improvement track and working only on big bangs. Both tracks are crucial to success.

Early Dual-Track Success at AT&T

It was 1986 and off-shore factories on the Pacific Rim were building telephone systems so fast and inexpensively that AT&T decided to close its business telephone manufacturing facility in Shreveport, Louisiana. The managers of the facility, however, convinced the company to give the operation one more chance. Aware that a mere incremental improvement would not provide the dynamics required to be successful, the managers selected our team from Coopers & Lybrand, with our relatively new two-track method, to assist them with their challenge.

The facility, Shreveport Works, wanted to install a traditional TQM process and develop a big bang project to get the foundering operation back on its feet as quickly as possible. The first step was to fast-track a restructuring of the entire production line using engineering optimization techniques. A traditional continuous improvement TQM initiative was also deployed. The initial engineering project was designed to get the manufacturing process cleaned up and to provide the data from which a real breakthrough or big bang opportunity could be identified. The two-track approach was the only process that held promise. There wasn't enough time for continuous improvement alone to bring the operation back to prominence.

The team discovered that the wave-soldering process used in making printed circuit boards produced an average of 4 defective boards out of every 10. From its research and intelligence work, the team also ascertained that all other companies engaged in this work used the same equipment. It was of the very latest design. Since these boards were required in every device manufactured at the facility, and since every other company using the process was experiencing the same rate of failure, it was decided that reengineering the circuit board manufacturing process would become the big bang challenge. "If we can beat them on the circuit board, we can win the race!" became the Shreveport Works' rallying cry.

By moving to a radically different technology and process of manufacturing and curing the circuit boards, Shreveport Works was able to virtually eliminate the production of defective boards. In less than 18 months it had reclaimed every production line that it had lost to the Asian manufacturers. Shreveport Works is now a primary source of the circuit board component for other AT&T manufacturers and even sells the components to other phone system manufacturers on the Pacific Rim.

In the case of Shreveport Works, survival was the prime driver. AT&T had given them one last chance to regain momentum. By integrating the activities required to address continuity and the activities required to meet the current crisis, Shreveport Works was better able to do both. Another factor in this success story was the leadership of the facility. Though motivated out of a sense of fear and survival, they did not let the magnitude of the challenge drive them down the path of familiarity. They looked to the future rather than to the past for answers. By taking a leap of faith, they were able to achieve an excellence beyond their own expectations and ensure long-term continuity for themselves and the facility. The plant continued to move incrementally forward with traditional TQM and to identify change challenges to address the future needs of the dynamic marketplace. Shreveport Works became a model for AT&T's improvement and strategic business processes.

As the two-track approach matured, it became apparent that the interests and success of a company are best served through an ongoing two-track methodology. By 1991 the management process had become informally recognized as the McArthur dual-track approach. The second, or break-through (big bang), track is now most often referred to as the reengineering track.

LEADERSHIP-DRIVEN

In successful management systems the leaders or senior staff are always the planning and decision-making body. In quality management this group is often called the quality steer-ing committee. We recommend it not be given a quality or other special identity. The planning group should simply be known as the senior committee or whatever the leadership group is currently called. Calling the group the quality steer-ing committee focuses on the process rather than the results. Improvement and change should be viewed as a way of life for the company, not a special effort. Only the senior group defines the mission for each team project, ensures that all information is pertinent and timely, and makes sure that everyone is properly educated for the tasks at hand.

STATISTICAL FOUNDATION

The value and importance of the statistical side of outcome management must not be minimized or trivialized. Under-standing processes, knowing variation theory and princi-ples, and having proficiency in data manipulation are extremely important to successful outcomes. We have learned through numerous TQM experiences, however, that most organizations of any magnitude already have individ-uals proficient in the use of these tools. It is therefore unnec-essary to wait for success until everyone can prepare a flow chart, Pareto diagram, or histogram. Just go ahead and do it! We recently encountered a training director who said that a senior officer of his firm should not attempt to direct a core process team until he was steeped in classical TQM training. That sounded suspiciously like someone protecting his turf.

In the scores of TQM and outcome management start-ups in which we have been involved, we have never recommended training a team until it had its mission. Then, and only then, do we assess the knowledge needs and provide the technical understanding required to activate the process. Statistical tools are best introduced when needed during live projects, not through training. Never underestimate the people you were smart enough to hire!

Deploying an advanced management system should pay off from day one. Maybe in the old seller's market there was time to ponder the moves, however, in the more dynamic buyer's market of today, time has become the most precious of all resources. Changing or advancing management methodologies must add value from the beginning. Go for the big bang.

The underlying premise of the dual-track approach to outcome management is that the same information used by the traditional process improvement teams can be used to create significant system redesign opportunities. Why not do both at the same time? Create cross-functional ad hoc breakthrough teams to work on big challenges, and with the same information, empower standing process teams to address issues at the process level. Lead and coordinate these activities from the top. Teamwork and collaboration are not synonyms. All work, including teamwork, must be performed in collaboration to truly benefit the system. The dual-track methodology, however, is only for addressing those issues that require a team effort.

THE DUAL-TRACK PROCESS

The dual tracks are a business track and an organization track. Figure 5 illustrates the two tracks. The business track

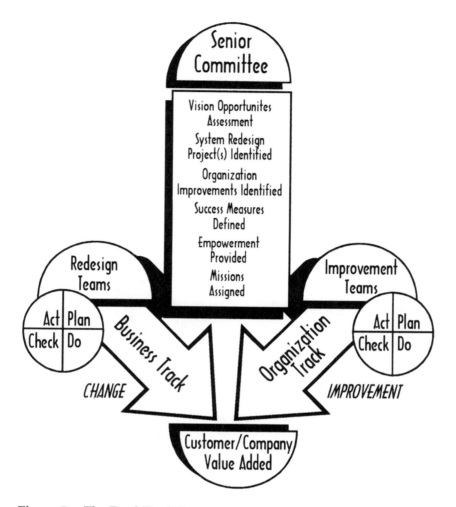

Figure 5. The Dual-Track Process

addresses issues and opportunities that will have a major impact on the customer and the business as a whole. The process used on the business track is key system redesign (or reengineering). Its missions are focused on improving or changing the business of the company. The organization track focuses on incremental process improvements in work processes, departments, and small, structured units. Whereas business track projects are carried out using cross-functional teams, organization track projects are usually addressed from within a particular process by an existing departmental team. The organization track addresses work (or organization) improvements, as with traditional TQM. The activities of both types of teams are led, directed, monitored, and commissioned by the senior staff or senior committee. The committee also ensures that the company's ongoing education and training needs are appropriately met. The senior committee functions in much the same way as an organization track team does. It has responsibility for constantly improving the project selection process for the successful integration of the outcome management system into the work of the company. The dual-track approach is focused on the teamwork aspect of collaboration. Keep in mind that the purpose of teamwork is to change and improve work. All work is not subject to teamwork, but all work must be collaborative to be of maximum value.

The senior committee commissions each business track system redesign mission and approves the projects selected by the organization track improvement teams. It also leads many of the assessments and data collection processes through close cooperation with the company's information technology function.

Here is an outline of a typical schedule for introducing the dual-track approach of outcome management to the workplace. Although this schedule is typical, the procedures described must be adapted to the prevailing culture of the company:

1. Assess

A. Planning:
- The senior committee meets to establish ground rules and a time for its regular meetings.

- The committee considers the general education, training, and data needs of the system redesign team members it will appoint and the continuous improvement teams that will be formed, and approves the basic curriculum for the teams and instructors, and the education schedule. The curriculum is determined by the knowledge and experience of those who will participate in the missions and the degree of difficulty of the various assignments. A typical curriculum includes group process knowledge, appropriate tools and techniques instruction, and an understanding of how the missions will add value for the customer and to the organization as a whole. The curriculum must be more than training; it must foster creative thought, include hands-on experiences, and be future focused.

B. Examining customers, products, services

- The committee appoints a vision review team to examine current and future customer relationships, current product reliability, service performance, and other pertinent data. Members of customer groups are invited to serve on this team, along with employees and staff. A committee member serves as the team leader.

- The vision review team prepares a written report describing the company's primary customers, products, and services in detail from both current and future perspectives. The report includes an assessment of how well the organization now meets or exceeds customer requirements and how those requirements might change in the future.

- The report is reviewed and approved by the senior committee.

C. Mapping work processes

- The senior committee appoints a systems pre-design team. This team, consisting of committee members and staff, develops a report mapping all the major work processes of the organization. The system report is provided to the vision review team, which then inventories and assesses current technology and examines organizational needs in relation to possible future needs.

- The systems pre-design team examines and reports on capacity use of the organization's processes. The report also describes supplier relationships.

- The report is reviewed and approved by the committee. When the assessment is complete, the committee revisits the vision and mission statements. Any immediate improvement opportunities, identified by the reports, are implemented and the first major system redesign project is selected. (Outsourced professionals are particularly useful during this phase.)

2. Plan

A. Establishing objectives
- The senior committee appoints an opportunities modeling team. Representatives of customer groups serve on the team, along with committee members and appropriate staff and other employees. The opportunities modeling team sets preliminary mission objectives for each system, function, or process that is under review for redesign or improvement.

B. Developing measures
- The opportunities modeling team develops a family of measures for each product or service and for system, function, and process performance. The measures for system redesign are drawn from the leadership's visioning and mission planning processes and knowledge gained from the reports. Quality, productivity, speed, and cost savings are the bases for the improvement measures.

- The opportunities modeling team recommends an ongoing organizationwide process measurement procedure. The procedure includes how, when, how often, and by whom the data will be collected and used.

3. Act

A. Establishing improvement and redesign projects

- The committee selects the improvement and redesign projects and assigns them to the appropriate teams. Customer representatives may be appointed to serve on selected teams.

- The teams are given training.

- The committee supplies each team with a mission statement and allocates the resources the team will need to execute its mission.

- Each team develops a work plan and submits it to the committee for review, adjustment, and approval.

- The committee approves or modifies the work plan and authorizes the team to proceed with the experiment.

B. Implementing the workplans

- The team implements the work plan using the eight-step P-D-C-A improvement cycle for improvement opportunities, or the advanced eight-step P-D-C-A system redesign cycle for system redesigns. (Both of these are explained in the following section.)

4. Review, Reward, and Recycle

- The committee evaluates the work of the teams, adopts the recommendations, or charges the team to repeat the experiment with recommended changes.

- The committee also evaluates the effectiveness of the organization's communication network and makes improvements if necessary.

- The achievements of each team are recognized and rewarded by the system. Each improvement and re-design is communicated and celebrated system wide.

- The committee develops a plan for deploying and expanding the entire continuous improvement and redesign process.

Using the dual-track approach ensures that all the opportunities of the company are addressed in an orderly and timely fashion, by the most appropriate parties. The reason many companies become disenchanted with TQM is that most deployment schemes travel solely on the organization track. Successful outcome management requires getting better and getting different at the same time—traveling on both tracks.

ORGANIZATION TRACK IMPROVEMENTS

The organization track is for addressing ongoing process and function improvements. The teams that work on improvement missions are most often standing teams within a process or a function. These teams meet on a regular basis to report on findings, monitor processes, address system relationships, and to model potential improvements of the processes for which they are accountable.

P-D-C-A IMPROVEMENT CYCLE

Traditional quality management and most improvement team (organization track) missions follow the scientific approach to problem solving—collect meaningful data, identify the root causes of the problem, identify appropriate solutions, and plan and make changes. One of the constants in the quality movement has been the use of the plan-do-check-act (P-D-C-A) cycle to address the last step in the scientific approach to problem solving—planning and making changes. Although advances in problem-solving software have accelerated and improved this process, the P-D-C-A cycle is still the basic tool used by organization track improvement teams. The version presented here and shown in Figure 6 is based on an eight-step version of the P-D-C-A cycle developed by Boise Cascade:

- Step 1. Understand the expectations of the customer. Every potential change is measured by the value it will add for the customer and to the company.

- Step 2. Determine and prioritize the intention of the process or function. "Why do we do this and why is it important?"

- Step 3. Map the process. In the old days, that meant hand-drawing a flow chart of the steps in the process. Today computers do that work for us.

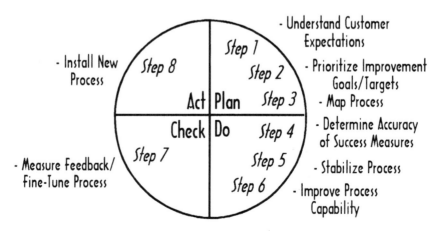

Figure 6.   Eight-Step Process Improvement P-D-C-A Cycle

- Step 4. Determine the accuracy of measures that have been set to identify a successful improvement.

- Step 5. Stabilize the process or eliminate variability within it.

- Step 6. Design an improvement for the process and run a test (usually on a small scale) to determine its potential for success.

- Step 7. Once the test is complete, assess feedback and fine-tune the new process.

- Step 8. Install the new process.

Some improvement projects are suggested by the senior committee and others by system managers. Most ideas for improving a process, however, come from those persons directly involved in it.

The idea or opportunity for improvement is then measured against the vision and value it will add to the customer/company measure. If there is no appropriate standing team to address the improvement opportunity, an ad hoc improvement team may be formed. Obviously it appoints persons involved in the process and others with special skills and knowledge to ensure success. Most improvement projects do not involve outside consultants but use in-house consultants to facilitate the work.

Once the process and causes of variation are thoroughly understood, an improvement is selected and the team works through the steps of the P-D-C-A improvement cycle.

IMPEDIMENTS TO IMPROVEMENT

The focus of improvement teams is improvement over time. The mission statements for improvement team projects include words like *realign, refine,* and *reduce.* The improvement process is a helix (see Figure 7). Each time a team completes the circle of the improvement process, it returns to the starting place wiser and on a higher level. The project may be different, but the goal is still the same— to reduce time, cost, and variation in the process to better serve the customer and the company.

The impediments to improvement are almost always cultural. Once an improvement team has received training in the fundamentals of problem solving and in working together, the members are emotionally and technically empowered to effect meaningful improvement.

If, however, the organization's leadership hasn't provided the spiritual empowerment, their work is doomed to failure. For example, if the company's reward system does not recognize the activity of the team as being as valuable as all other work, the team will sacrifice success to ensure that the more important work is addressed.

Besides the cultural impediment, success can also be hampered by flawed communication from management (e.g., an unclear mission), inadequate or too-early training, and technological barriers beyond the scope of the teams. If

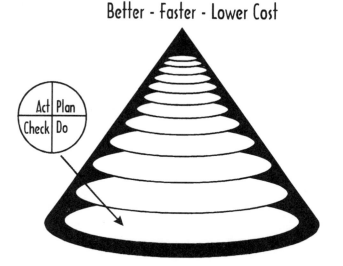

Figure 7.   Improvement Process Helix

the senior committee takes its job seriously, these impediments will be overcome in the diagnostic and planning phases of implementation.

The early work of the improvement teams can be called picking the low fruit. In most any department there is enough low fruit to be picked to ensure that the new effort produces some early successes, however, neither the committee nor the various teams must allow themselves to be unwittingly seduced by early success. The low fruit could probably be picked without using the tools and techniques of outcome management, but using these techniques helps determine which fruit to pick first and why and provides hands-on experience that will prove valuable when addressing more difficult challenges. As stated before, these early improvement successes provide an opportunity to celebrate the initiative and communicate the potential companywide.

The standing improvement teams meet on a regular basis to evaluate progress, review data, and to plan, prioritize, and recommend future projects. Early on, the projects are assigned by the committee. Later the improvement teams participate in the selection of projects and develop their own projects—in accordance with the company's overall vision.

CHAPTER 5

Big Bangs—System Redesign

"The empires of the future are the empires of the mind."

—Winston Churchill

REDESIGN? REENGINEERING? INNOVATION?

The process that we call system redesign has myriad names, including reengineering, core process redesign, business systems redesign, and process innovation. There is no difference in the intent or in the basic philosophies of each of these views. Do not allow yourself to be confused. It appears that Michael Hammer's title for the process—Reengineering—has become the most popular.

We define a process as the actual work that is required to produce a specific output. A function is a collection of related work processes. And a system is a key operation of the company made up of functions and processes; hence our use of the term *system redesign*. System redesign is the procedure that is followed on the business track of the dual-track approach.

In outcome management most of the company's energies and resources are dedicated to the dual-track's business track or to system redesign. System redesign is not new; however, in recent years, it has become more accessible and less difficult to execute because of advancing technologies. Data gathering, simulation options, and technology applications have been simplified through technological advances.

The major difference between our concept and those presented by most of our colleagues is the use of the dual-track approach—that is, the retention of the incremental improvement-focused organization track. Many of these other philosophies treat organization track activities as a given. We are concerned, though, that many in leadership roles misunderstand the value in traveling on both tracks when the concept is not presented in tandem. Still, it is the system redesign projects on the business track that will move the organization to significantly higher performance, productivity, and profits.

BIG BANG EXAMPLE

The introduction of the dual-track methodology must begin with a big bang redesign project. When Glaxo Technical Operations in the Research Triangle near Raleigh, North Carolina, began its *Glaxo Excellence Process* (their name for outcome management), they selected a "doozie" for their big bang redesign kickoff project. Glaxo is the world's second largest pharmaceutical company. Therefore, the redesign project selected to deploy its quality system through the dual-track approach was a mammoth and complex challenge with the potential for a significant payoff.

At issue was the manufacturing and distribution of a product that was in great demand during the cold season. The demand varies by season; the shelf-life of the product is limited; and manufacturing of the product depends on a number of internal and external factors as well as close communication between marketing and purchasing. The information logistics were very complex. "If we can lick this problem through a quality management process," suggested a senior vice-president, "there's no challenge beyond our reach."

A team of highly skilled, self-motivated, and knowledgeable senior staffers was commissioned to reduce manufacturing and distribution lead time by one-third over the next five years at a yet-to-be-determined significant cost savings. A time goal of six months was established for the project. It was determined that the data collection and manipulation processes would take too long using traditional methods, so the group outsourced a process-modeling software package to support the effort.

After three months, it was obvious the team was onto something. Through much debate, discussion, and some fighting among themselves and with others, the first pass at the redesign indicated a total cost savings of $20 million and a lead-time reduction from 103 days to 60 days. The final results were a savings of more than $30 million and a lead-time reduction to 18 days in the fifth year. Other accomplishments identified by the team were dramatic increases in customer satisfaction, personal job enrichment through the collaborative process, increased quality process credibility, and significant increases in advanced skills by each member of the team. Once the results of the study were announced, the quality director was besieged by the team's co-workers, demanding their turn to ride on the Glaxo quality train!

COMPONENTS OF REDESIGN

There are six key components to successful system redesign that we have confirmed through experience and logic:

- System redesign has always played a part in successful quality and outcome management systems as the procedure for the business track in the dual-track approach.

- An aggressive and intentional approach is essential for system redesign to work.

- Information and information technology are powerful tools for enabling and implementing system redesign.

- All organizational resources, especially human resources, must be marshaled and organized in support of a system redesign project.

- System redesign must occur within an overall strategic context and be guided by a vision from the organization's leader.

- For the company to gain full value from the effort, the results of the system redesign must also be applied to all other functions and processes.

Each of these is discussed in the following sections.

System redesign has always played a part in successful quality and outcome management systems as the procedure for the business track of the dual-track approach. The radical change of business performance is rooted in the dual-track approach. Traditional quality management, however, focused mostly on the incremental improvement track. This focus on continuous improvement over radical change was often effective for the times and the tempo of business. When the marketplace became more turbulent, competitive, and customer focused, the demand for radical business change intensified. Outcome management focuses on the change track because of the ongoing need to change work to address ever-shifting business requirements.

An aggressive and intentional approach is essential for system redesign. Breakthroughs do not occur in a cavalier manner. The effort must be structured, commissioned, and fully supported by the company's leadership. The project will not be successful if it is handed off to a subordinate group. Total leadership involvement is required. The leadership must select the project, give it structure, provide the enablers, clearly articulate the project's mission (in concert with the overall vision), and participate in the redesign effort.

Information and information technology are powerful tools for enabling and implementing system redesign. Although it is theoretically possible to bring about radical change without the aid of computers, there are no cited examples that we have found. Information technology is an enabler that captures current activity and provides modeling and simulations of potential ideal systems to meet the redesign challenge. Information technology is also the implementer, becoming a part of the new design and the process by which the redesign is installed. The question is not, "To automate or not to automate?" It is, "After we've simplified, combined, and eliminated all non-value-added activity (work) . . . how do we automate what's left?"

The opportunities from the application of information technology take a variety of forms:

- Automation—Eliminating human labor from the process.

- Sequencing—Changing the sequence of a process, or performing tasks in parallel.

- Geographic—Enabling processes to operate effectively over long distances.

- Disintermediation—Eliminating process intermediaries and non-value-added steps.

All organizational resources, especially human resources, must be marshaled and organized in support of a system redesign project. How people are organized and directed as well as the degree to which they are empowered to perform and improve their work are critical to successful system redesign. Specific organizational and human resource approaches likely to facilitate the redesign process include empowering workers to handle entire processes (particularly at the customer interface), establishing autonomous work teams, and creating new, more process-oriented organizational structures. Such actions typically work in concert with information technology.

Organizational and human resources are essential because the outcome of system redesign is radical cultural change as well as radical process change. Roles will change along with processes (work). The organization must be ready to accept change. Preparedness for change begins with a clear mandate from leadership to accept change or suffer the consequences. System redesign is not a management public relations effort. It is serious, risky business. If the leaders make it clear that change and collaboration will be the drivers of reward, change and collaboration will become standard operating procedures.

System redesign must occur within an overall strategic context and be guided by a vision from the top. The formulation of a strategy and a mission for the system redesign must emanate from the vision set forth by the leader. Without the strategy-vision connection, the project will become a traditional TQM, or incremental, improvement. There should be no distinction between the leadership vision, the strategic plan, the marketing plan, and system redesign. The purpose of system redesign is to allow the company to dramatically differentiate itself from the competition and to attract more sales and customers. System redesign is not industrial engineering. It's marketing!

For the company to gain full value from the effort, the results of the system redesign must also be applied to all other functions and processes. System redesign has a high initial cost in time, money, and human resources. Part of the initial cost can be quickly regained by applying the lessons learned in the design phase to other systems, functions, and processes.

How to apply the lessons learned from the effort should be an intentional part of the redesign plan.

CRITICAL SUCCESS FACTORS

For a redesign project to succeed, the company's leadership must be fully committed to the effort and to the implementation of the redesign. Success also depends on a well-defined project mission with a clear scope, parameters, and a desired outcome. The project must have a specific duration and the full commitment of such resources as time, money, people, and technology. Leadership must select the best-qualified players for the redesign team. The team must be of a manageable size—usually no more than 10 members—to ensure flexibility, creativity, and effectiveness. The role of each member must be clearly defined, and there must be rules of procedure and accountability. Communication with leadership and other stakeholders must be continuous and often. The team must be appropriately educated and trained. Good facilities, the best tools, and full company support are also prerequisites. The corporate culture must allow the team to think outside the box. No process, function, task, territory, or system is sacred. Everything must be subject to change, improvement, or elimination.

Systems are dynamic and changing. Even the possibility of redesigning a system produces an effect or a change upon it. There is no future in the past. That's why the redesign process focuses on systems thinking rather than systems analysis of past efforts. The redesign process must leap first to the future for ideals and models. Systems analysis is at best a stimulus and one of many data points of consideration.

Because of the dynamics of business systems, it is important that redesign teams have great freedom of thought. There is no one solution but an infinite spectrum of options. Redesign teams must be equipped to think and function in several dimensions at one time. They must recognize the ambiguities of all things and apply each lesson learned as they move to and from the future. The single rule of decision making for the redesign team is the same rule applied by leaders with mettle and conviction—We'll do it if it feels right. Great redesigns spring forth from an uncommon group common sense driven by the members' spirit, emotions, and feelings, not from mechanical processes like calculation and scientific deduction.

KEY SYSTEMS DEFINED

To review our model of a company: the two basic parts are a company's organization and its business. Business is the outcome of work. The organization is the structure in which work takes place. Work takes place in processes, functions, and systems. Systems are the key operations of the company. In our own consulting group client satisfaction, the securement of engagements, the continuing education and enlightenment of our practitioners, and business administration are our primary systems. All other activities, processes, and functions support these four key systems. Each system also has an owner—one person who is responsible for leading and managing the activities within the system.

Glaxo Pharmaceuticals has identified its key systems as product launch, process management, distribution, supplier management, information management, and worker empowerment.

Processes are improved, consolidated, or eliminated. Functions are simplified and integrated. Processes and functions are addressed on the incremental improvement organization track. Systems are created and redesigned and are addressed by cross-functional teams on the business track.

SYSTEM REDESIGN PROCEDURE

System redesign begins with leadership's painting a picture of a desired future drawn from their understanding of the needs of the future. The redesign project is based on the assumption that better is no longer a practical goal. Companies that waste time just getting better risk being destroyed by a competitor who searches creatively for a radically different way to serve the customer.

The second step in system redesign is to identify the current key systems and then select the one for redesign that will have the greatest impact on the demands of the customer and the profitability of the company. Identifying key systems and selecting one for redesign are made very difficult with cultural and turf issues. Not everyone will understand the value of multilevel systems thinking and will therefore attempt to protect turf and territory. That's why many companies must carefully examine their reward systems. Multilevel thinking requires true loyalty to the system. Not everyone will be loyal to the system. System redesign requires collaboration and trust of the highest order. If the company's current formal and informal rewards system does not reward the kind of behaviors required to move the organization to a new level of performance, the reward system must be changed.

The third step is for the redesign team to examine the array of tools and technologies that are available to bring maximum success to the redesign, to map current activity, to collect pertinent data from inside and outside the company (customers and competition), and to develop a preliminary ideal model through system simulations.

Most companies in today's marketplace have bought into the idea that their business strategy must be driven by a marketing strategy, not a financial strategy. These same companies are, for the most part, also engaged in some type of continuous improvement process, whether they call it TQM or not. Traditional TQM projects promise improvements in the range of 15 to 30 percent. Not bad if your competition is sitting still. But if a big bang system redesign doesn't produce a gain of 100 percent or better, the effort may be a bust.

Most companies still use past performance to measure success and to plan for the future. Some have become more sophisticated and use current performance as the measure of success and the basis of planning. Outcome management sets measures in the future—in another dimension. The idea is to select targets for which there are no current measures. The question then becomes, "How are we *going* to do?" not "How did we do?" or "How are we doing?"

DEFINING A REDESIGN PROJECT

The first question to ask when attempting to establish a system redesign project is, "How could we do things differently?" This question pertains to the interconnected relationships of the customer, the company, the key systems, and the future. Once the mission is established, the question becomes, "How will the new system work?" That means what would the ideal system look like and perform like in terms of flow, output, boundaries, performance, organization, and technology? The question to ask in setting up performance measures and objectives is, "How well will it work?" Cost, quality, cycle-time, and responsiveness are the measures. When identifying the factors critical to the redesign's success you must ask the question, "What things have to go right?" People, technology, product, and process are the factors. The last question in the project identification stage is, "Why might things not go right?" The list of answers includes resource allocation, technical issues, product factors, market/environmental issues, and the most important of all—cultural and organizational political issues.

P-D-C-A REDESIGN CYCLE

The P-D-C-A cycle for redesign shown in Figure 8 is future driven, whereas the improvement P-D-C-A cycle is usually driven by a current need or challenge. The senior committee carefully and thoughtfully sets the mission for a system redesign. Most companies will attempt only one or two system redesigns at a time and no more than two per year. The P-D-C-A redesign cycle has the following eight steps:

- Step 1. Establish a business-driven mission.

- Step 2. Address all cultural barriers to the project's success.

- Step 3. Establish the project's critical success factors, including the creation of a corporate culture that allows the redesign team to think and act outside the box. The team must also be appropriately trained, educated, and equipped.

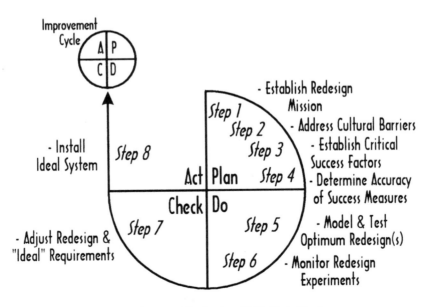

Figure 8. Eight-Step System Redesign P-D-C-A Cycle

- Step 4. Define what an ideal system should look like and how it might perform, and create the metric or measures of success.

- Step 5. Model and test optimum redesigns against the ideal.

- Step 6. Monitor the redesign experiment.

- Step 7. Adjust the redesigns and ideal requirements.

- Step 8. Install the ideal system.

Once installed, the new system becomes subject to the improvement P-D-C-A cycle. Along the way any lessons learned that might be useful to improve other systems, functions, and processes are recognized and deployed. The activities that make up the P-D-C-A redesign cycle are, for the most part, technology driven.

BOTTLENECKS AND BREAKTHROUGHS

Webster describes a bottleneck as "a condition or situation that retards or halts free movement and progress." Obviously it takes more than an improvement to make it through a bottleneck. That's why the early big bang projects are important when installing an outcome management system and when addressing other dynamic business issues. A significant early breakthrough is a valuable change agent. In the early stage of installing the new management philosophy it is important that the effort be recognized as serious. Since redesign teams include persons from across the organization, the opportunity to communicate the value of the new initiative is greater than with a departmentally-focused improvement project.

A breakthrough on the business track produces dramatic change, thereby affecting the outcome of business and life throughout the company. When real change becomes recognized as a welcomed agent in the corporate culture, resistance to change from the various constituencies diminishes.

The work of the redesign teams becomes even more important and difficult as time passes. It is from these big bangs, however, that the company grows, prospers, and comes closest to its vision. The change produced by improvement teams is incremental rather than significant. Improvement teams improve processes, serve as training ground for redesign teams, and provide the senior committee with suggestions for potential systems redesign missions.

Bottlenecks are most often created by culture. Even in some organizations that have been successful with TQM, there is a hidden loyalty to the old ways. Some leaders give lip service to the concept of change, yet find incremental improvement more to their liking. Improvement is obviously easier to lead than is change. Change is a stressor; it requires coping. "The old way is dying and something new is taking its place—how will it affect me, us, them?" Change demands explanation—that is, communication—if it is to become integrated into the system. The biggest bottlenecks to successful deployment usually lie near the top, with vice-presidents and directors who don't believe the change will really take or who are afraid that their influence will diminish under the new management style. Those who are compliant, yet appear to be on board, represent the greatest bottlenecks to success.

Another bottleneck to system redesign is resource allocation—determining the best use of the money, time, and people available to address the most appropriate challenges. Making these decisions within a company that is driven by outcome is difficult at best. But imagine what it must be like in those organizations yet to hear or believe the quality message. Resource allocation is a primary function of the senior committee.

A friend and client in the healthcare industry encourages everyone in his organization to share every idea, no matter how outlandish or costly it might at first appear. He says, "Everything is possible, at a cost, but possible. Many of our greatest accomplishments were introduced as impossible to do, but . . . ."

SUCCESS BREEDS DISCONTENT

The biggest problem encountered with early redesign projects is created by success. The CEO has truly empowered the troops, giving them the knowledge, information, tools, and culture they need to change and improve work. The redesign team has set its mission and its course. Now the leader, in the words of Tom Peters, "is in control, because he is out of control." In fact, now the leaders don't know everything that's going on. They don't need to. Others are now making the decisions that they were once called upon to make.

Enter the naysayers, those who appear to be on board but have been waiting secretly for the whole thing to come apart. They start asking leaders what's going on, and they can't answer them as succinctly as they could in the past. They get anxious, shifts back into the control mode, and wants to know more about what's going on. The team gets frustrated because they can feel the culture moving away from the collaborative environment they need, back to the old control mentality they do not need for continued success.

On another front, the support groups like the training department, human resources, and the financial people, those who are not yet fully linked to the key system redesign team and the redesign effort, begin to question certain aspects of the redesign plan and to create bottlenecks to the project by questioning the basic assumptions on which the proposed redesign is based.

The best solution to this difficult problem is prevention. One of the early goals of a redesign effort must be the creation of a formal link among all parties affected by the proposed change.

Let's look at this issue through the redesign of a supply chain key system. Supply chain management means taking care of business from concept to the consumption of a product or service as a system, not as a series of processes. Instead of organizing work vertically, by department, work is reorganized horizontally, by customer need. There are three natural stages in the redesign of a typical supply chain:

- In stage one the management mission focuses primarily on logistics—controlling the flow of output from the various links of the chain. Cooperation in this phase is usually very high, because not much has changed from a functional point of view. Integration, however, is beginning to occur.

- In stage two there is a shift from logistics to tactics, and the redesigned process begins to integrate functions like customer service and order processing. The need for cooperation continues to increase as more territories become integrated instead of just linked.

- In stage three, the logistics and tactics of supply chain management become driven solely by the company's business strategy or by its missions. Integration reaches the point at which functions literally disappear. That's scary if you are a department or function head. You begin to wonder if you're going to be needed when the redesign is complete.

To address this important and fundamental issue of the integration of work, one of our clients created the following mission for its key system redesign team: to improve the team's capability to build an advanced supplier-customer partnering model that integrates logistics, communications, and transactions. Achieving full cooperation from persons whose jobs are changing or may even be eliminated is no easy task. The next best way of dealing with the issues of linkage and integration, if the preventive measures were absent or didn't hold, is to revisit the vision that started all this emphasis on change in the first place. Revisiting the leader's "I wants" is often particularly useful in getting the leader back on track. The naysayers will often come around when they become confident that the leader is holding to the new course.

PROCESS OF CHAMPIONS

The system redesign concept requires a higher level of knowledge in specific disciplines—advanced engineering, psychology, statistics, chemistry, and technologies. Therefore, insufficient education and preparation can also be a bottleneck to progress. Some organizations train key individuals to work as in-house consultants to team projects; others rely on outsourcing when specialties are needed.

An approach to growing knowledgeable in-house consultants and team members that we've found to be effective is our Five-Step champions knowledge transfer process, which is illustrated in Figure 9. When the complex challenges of redesigning a key system are being addressed, it is important to develop internal experts in techniques and methodologies—process champions. The knowledge transfer process is led by subject matter experts from outside the organization and uses a teaching methodology that integrates learning with the actual application of the knowledge gained. The champions process includes:

Classroom:

- **Theory**—Understanding of and education in advanced methodologies, technologies, and tech-

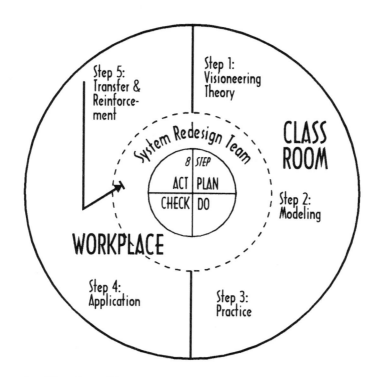

Figure 9. Five-Step Champions Knowledge Transfer Process

niques taught by content mentors (i.e., subject matter experts).

- **Modeling**—Demonstrations of concepts and techniques using pertinent examples from the company's work environment.

- **Practice**—Addressing specific opportunities and challenges from the work environment through homework and case studies.

Workplace:

- **Application**—Champions move into the workplace to activate the knowledge transfer and to pass it along through an apprenticeship process.

- **Advancement**—Champions work with content mentors for reinforcement of the subjects learned and to acquire deeper knowledge through in-process mentoring.

Determining which processes need a breakthrough, where the greatest potentials for redesign breakthroughs are, and making a cost/value analysis are the responsibilities of the senior staff. They must, though, ask the question, "Anybody got any good ideas?" and be receptive to the responses. It is in this type of collaborative environment that breakthroughs are possible and do occur.

Redesign teams are special groups, representing various skills and talents, organized to effect change in business. These teams examine new ideas, concepts, and technologies to find a new way to impact the outcome of the business. Their goal is to change the company and move performance to a higher level.

CHAPTER 6

Before You Start—Deploying Outcome Management

"Be sure you're right; then go ahead."

—Davy Crockett

PATIENCE IS STILL A VIRTUE

The key to successful deployment of outcome management and the Dual-Track methodology is patience before you start and impatience from there on out. Make sure all the leaders and those who serve in other key positions have a clear understanding of what is about to happen and are ready to truly work together.

Successful management systems are built on a family model rather than on a military model; on making wisdom available throughout the organization—not just at the top; on having people working and thinking in collaboration rather than in layers; and from a single focus on meeting the customer's and the company's needs—not on organizational politics and personal agendas. Successful management systems are also home grown and are rarely built on a "follow our dots" program like those available from some quality consultants, accounting firms, or business schools.

In a typical path of successful deployment, the leader or leaders first become interested in developing a new management philosophy or advancing the current one, and then seek a deeper understanding of the many concepts reported in business magazines and books—concepts like total quality management, reengineering, core process redesign, and outcome management. They gain understanding by reading, attending seminars, and talking with knowledgeable peers. The next step is to find a coach or a mentor. Some leaders hire or appoint a staff member to serve in that capacity. Others retain a consultant or rely on a personal relationship with a colleague.

Once the leaders are reasonably comfortable with their level of understanding, they along with the coach conduct an informal analysis of the organization's potential for accepting a philosophical change. This analysis then serves as the basis for the design of a preliminary deployment strategy. That strategy usually begins with an effort to create an awareness and understanding of the new management concepts in the senior staff.

By the time the senior staff reaches sufficient understanding, the leader, with the aid of the coach, prepares to introduce the new philosophy into the company's planning process. The annual planning activity usually serves as the point of introduction. Prior to the planning activity, however, the leadership has commissioned data-gathering projects such as customer surveys and organizational culture and process assessments.

Armed with this valuable information, the leader develops a vision. The senior staff then develops new company missions based on the vision and establishes projects to address them. Organization improvement teams are formed to address the routine process improvement opportunities, and a system redesign team is appointed to manage a significant big bang project to get the initiative off to a grand start. The core leadership group reviews the results of the team projects and then communicates the successes of the efforts throughout the organization. The deployment of the new management philosophy (outcome management) is underway.

This scenario of leadership's identifying improvement opportunities and redesign projects, and establishing and empowering teams, is repeated again and again until the new philosophy disappears and becomes the company's accepted management style. True outcome management, or any management philosophy, should have no separate identity. It should be business as usual.

Deploying an outcome management system does, however, require considerable effort, attention, and resources. There is information to be collected and shared, activities to be communicated, and lessons to be learned. It is the role of the coach or consultant to provide proven processes, point out possible barriers, and ensure that the leaders stay on the appropriate path—not to provide shortcuts and side trips. Early in the rollout, the consultant or coach may facilitate certain meetings and activities but with the goal of teaching others within the organization to assume the responsibility as soon as possible.

The coach should also have assessment tools that can be modified to meet the organization's particular needs. Training may also be provided by the consultant or coach, but only at the time of need and specific to the task at hand. For example, being able to read a process flow chart is necessary. It is better to teach flow charting, however, by using the actual work flow in which the employee regularly participates instead of some abstract activity like making a cup of coffee. The role of the consultant or coach throughout the deployment process is to mentor the leaders, not to personally lead the effort themselves or get in its way. Consultants and coaches should be heard and not seen.

Outcome management is a path that begins with awareness and understanding, moving to empowerment, and on to deployment. The leader goes first and the others in the organization follow, moving from the top down (see Figure 10).

Successful management systems are never built from the bottom up. Outcome management, like other management systems, requires a culture change in order to be

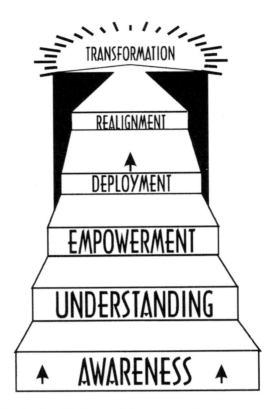

Figure 10. Deploying Outcome Management

effectively implemented. No one in the organization will accept the new philosophy until he or she are convinced the leaders are totally committed to the effort. Money spent on skills enhancement before commitment is wasted. Time and the resources for conducting an employee suggestion program before the employees know what the customer really wants go right down the drain. Packaged programs and how-to seminars at business schools never work until there is direction and commitment from the top.

It is far worse to play at management change than it is to have no management philosophy at all—especially if you're playing some outside consultant's game. Take your time before you start. Learn what you can on your own. Find a coach, not a program. Develop your own plan and go for it. Any kind of quality-based management system is a powerful creative tool in the hands of a knowledgeable craftsperson. It can wreak havoc in the hands of a part-time tinkerer.

FUTURE-FOCUSED WORKS!

The primary role of leadership in outcome management is to provide challenging and rewarding missions within the organization to address the changing demands and needs of the customer and the company and to create the right attitude toward work and change. Processes, functions, and systems are managed, improved, redesigned, or eliminated according to the needs of the business. People are empowered with whatever they need to get the job done. The organization serves the needs of business; form follows function. The culture of the company must be collaborative and always welcome to change. That kind of culture is only possible if the leadership provides a reward system that demands collaboration and openness to change.

In outcome management planning begins with, "What do we want?" not, "What can we make out of what we have?" Knowledge and technology are the drivers of outcome management and the strategy is to address business opportunities and organizational improvements simultaneously on two parallel tracks. The methodology is the dual-track approach that is led and managed by the top people in the organization. These leaders provide the vision and missions, the knowledge, information, tools, and culture with which everyone can perform and improve work.

For some companies the problem is not being unable to see the future, it's being unable to let go of the past. Peter Drucker suggests to his clients that they make a list of all the things they are doing today that, if not already being done, wouldn't be begun. And he further suggests that they use the list to do away with unnecessary practices. All companies are burdened with a commitment, a process, an investment, a structure, or a policy that does not add value for the customer or the company. Yet abandoning it is very difficult because the condition is woven into the organization's culture.

It is crucial to success to begin in the future, with a vision, then apply Drucker's exercise. Don't begin the process of renewal by reflecting on the past. You'll find more useless procedures and practices if you begin with the future in mind.

SECTION II

Aim. The Basis of Unconventional Thinking

"The most beautiful thing we can experience is the mysterious. It is the source of all true art and science."

—Albert Einstein

THINKING ABOUT EVERYTHING

A recurring theme of this book is the reminder to: Dream before you think, think before you plan, and plan before you act. We have also introduced the need for leaders and managers to look at issues and opportunities with a system view, rather than through a myopic focus on a particular process or function, to understand the interrelatedness of all things. Another theme is that there is no future in the past. By imaging a desired outcome from the future, it is easier to design the ideal system to achieve it. In this section we will provide strategies and structures through which proposed outcomes, futures, ideal systems, and visions should be filtered and assessed.

The occasional stories throughout the book are obviously there to strengthen a point. But more important, the stories have been included to show how to find useful knowledge from nontraditional sources. You are encouraged to go back to these stories to look for ideas, thoughts, and connections that might prove useful as you attempt to unconventionalize your thinking. These stories are also included to raise your comfort level in looking to the future for challenges.

STANDING AT THE EDGE

When we come to the edge we have reached a frontier. We know instinctively that the present holds the promise of change. Though change is not always a welcome state, when we stand on the edge we feel the anxiety of its inevitability. Even if we choose to go back, we are different—or changed—for having stood at the edge.

Thinkers, tinkerers, and artists live and work on the edges of their cultures. They know instinctively that change—new ideas, gadgets, expressions, and chemistries —springs forth from the ambiguity, the randomness, and the chaos found at the edge or beyond.

When we operate only from the middle of a culture, it is impossible to know the fullness and richness of it. All of our ideas, decisions, and judgments are drawn solely from the past and the present. All of our observations are from a centered perspective only. Going over the same territory again and again, without venturing out, creates a false sense of adequacy that can grow until it knows no bounds.

Though it is at the edge where real innovations are discovered, most business endeavors discourage working or thinking too close to the edge. Everyone is expected to stay close to the center.

If working at the edge empowers the poet, the artist, and the scientist, why not the business leader? Is there a difference in the process of commerce and other thought-

ful endeavors that renders unconventional thinking use-less? Organizations are just like any other living sys-tems—they are what they perceive themselves to be, to one degree or another. If the only image of the organiza-tion is that which can be seen only from the center, that image is the sole source of reference for creating, plan-ning, and acting.

The Buddha pointed out long ago that we are what we think. "Every civilization, whether it is spiritual, scien-tific, or material," said the Buddha, "is merely an exter-nalization of consciousness." It is therefore important for us to think of our work culture in a holistic manner—as a combination of spirit, science, and the material.

If an organization's leaders do not give value to the whole of the system, if they honor the material, the spirit, or science over the other important cultural components, business opportunities will be minimized and mediocrity will drive the company's vision.

Just as the artist and scientist must search for ideas and concepts at the edges of their worlds, so must the leaders of commerce. The goal of any creator is the same: to manifest an elegant innovation with a purpose that cel-ebrates change.

Therefore, for art to inspire, science to enrich, and business to prosper, there must be a proper mixture of the material, of spirit, and of science.

Outcome management demands that leaders be cre-ators—to think innovatively, multidimensionally, and unconventionally. It also demands that leaders go fre-quently to the edge for wisdom and to empower those they lead to do the same. The future is visible only from the edge; it cannot be seen from the center of the organiza-tion's culture. The center contains the present, which is a product of the past.

When we move to the edge, we approach the familiar from a new angle, and we see a different shape. The com-pany and its vision don't change, but our perspective of them does, thus adding new wisdom to complement our experiences and our centered observations. At the frontier, the organization may no longer appear linear; it may look round. Where we once saw it as a machine, it may now appear to be a cog in a bigger machine. Where we once saw it to be a single system, it may become a process in a larger system. By empowering ourselves and those with whom we work to stand at the edge, we broaden the horizon of thought, expand the opportunities of creativity, and provide a different picture of the present.

Dreaming, thinking, planning, and acting in the outcome management environment require unconventionality. Conventional dreaming and thinking lead to the ordinary. The ordinary will get you nowhere. Planning and acting in the same old ways are at best regressive. There is no future in the past. And it is only from the edge that the reality of a promising future can be seen and unconventional thinking can occur.

The outcome management process is driven by visions—visions created by fearless leaders who risk the impossible, think the unthinkable, and empower all others to do the same; by leaders who lead from the edge of the culture as well as from its center.

CHAPTER 7

Integrating—
Unconventional Thinking

"Thinking is not simply the description—by perception or recall—of something which is there. It is the use of information . . . to get somewhere else."

—F.C. Bartlett

STRUCTURE AND STRATEGIES

Section I was devoted primarily to attitude—one of the five business success factors. It provides ways to identify the right attitude, nourish it, and use it to achieve the vision of the company's leaders and address the daily work and special missions of the company. Section II addresses the two other business success factors that can be influenced by the company's leaders—structure and strategies—and provides an understanding of the new way of thinking required to achieve success through the outcome management philosophy. The factors that can't be influenced by leaders are the changing demands of the customer and the business ecosystem.

The six components of structure are futures, mission, value, success factors, measures, and synergistic actions. The seven strategies, to be discussed later in the section, are technology planning, time reduction, quality discipline, knowledge culture, competitive fitness, activity-based costing and system redesign (presented in chapter 5).

Structure Components

The structure components are the key elements of a meaningful planning process and serve as a filter or checklist for all planning to ensure that the desired outcome or mission is clear and adds significant value. The list is also used to evaluate work. The six components and the questions that must be answered to ensure that the organization's missions and work are relevant are:

- Future—Have all the important potential futures been considered in establishing this change or improvement mission? Who knows the answer? How do they know?

- Mission—Is this mission clear and worth the effort? Who created this mission and why?

- Value—How does this mission or activity add value or eliminate non-value in the system? Is this activity in synchronization with the vision and the principles of the company.

- Success Factors—How will the customer be better served by this effort? How will life in the company improve?

- Measures—Do we have sufficient measures to ensure that we know when the mission is achieved or the activity improved? Are the measures valid and easy to understand?

- Synergistic Actions—How will this effort improve collaboration, maximize the use of corporate resources and core competencies, and promote the system view?

All planning must be filtered through these six structure components to provide a common platform from which to evaluate, change, and improve work. Answering these questions as a part of the planning process increases the potential for successfully elevating the opportunity for improvement or change beyond the ordinary. Using the structure checklist should become routine for everyone involved in planning improvements and change.

A company planning group answered the questions this way:

Future: "The planning group will proceed to create change without considering sacred cows; there are none in the company. All work and every individual must add value for the customer and the company." (A mandate from the CEO.)

Mission: "The company's reward system will be based on collaboration by January 1995." This mission reflects the senior committee's commitment to provide a workplace that celebrates diversity and rewards collaboration.

Value: "In support of our collaborative spirit, any promise made to a customer by anyone in the organization will be met at any cost."

Success Factors: "We will know that the mission is successful when the new reward system is installed and operating to the satisfaction of management and employees."

Measures: "Reduced operating expenses, higher productivity, happier customers, and improved cooperation will be the primary measures of the success of this mission."

Synergistic Actions: "Operational accounting functions and routine human resource activities will be conducted at the key system level and will no longer be full administrative functions. The heads of these departments will become in-house consultants to the managers of key business systems."

When all planning and actions are filtered through these six structure components, the whole system becomes self-renewing—feeding on itself, gaining strength, and changing with each lesson learned. Establish the right attitude, build a foundation of knowledge, technology, and strategy that supports good planning, and the future will become clearer and more easily achievable.

THINKING CHANGES

The shift from the seller's market of the 1960s and 1970s to the buyer's market of today caused a shift from a tactical emphasis in marketing to a strategic emphasis—thinking versus acting. The work of the leaders also shifted from managing success to planning success. Whereas the CEO in the old business setting focused most of his thinking on manipulating the numbers and conserving resources, the new business setting requires thinking about the future as it relates to the customer. What will the customer want? Where will the customer be? Why will the customer want to do business with us? What must we create or change to meet the needs of our customer and the needs of our company?

Thinking in the old business setting was often based solely on experience, and often narrow, focused, and directed to a single issue. Creativity from the front office was usually drawn from experience, memory, and the learned accomplishments of others. "Let me put my mind to it," said the CEO, "and I'll give you my answer tomorrow."

This single-issue thinking was tactical by nature. The implications or downstream or upstream effects of management decisions were often given only cursory consideration. When the pace of business quickened and the dynamics of change accelerated, the need for multidimensional or strategic thinking increased. In the old days, it often consumed less time and fewer resources and was more politically expedient to just fix the effects of a problem rather than try to eliminate its root cause. As the demands on time and resources increased, and the costs associated with them increased, so did the need to eliminate root causes altogether.

The complexities and the future focus of outcome management require a shift from myopic thinking and planning to multilevel, multisubject thinking.

MORE WITH LESS

The theme of business in the 1990s is doing more with less. Each year new tools are introduced with the promise of answering the more with less challenge. Some of the supposedly new tools are merely reinventions or improvements of old ones; others are fads and gimmicks; while some are truly new and innovative and hold great promise.

For example, the seven strategies—technology, culture, competitive fitness, activity-based costing, time, quality, and system redesign—were selected from the numerous strategies that are available to business leaders. We think these seven are the most useful for meeting today's challenges. Doing more with less doesn't, however, mean changing from one strategy or tool to another; it means selecting the right tool at the right time and integrating the use of that tool with all the other activities of the company. Our seven strategies or tools are basic to the leader's toolbox. Every time another strategy is considered, deployed, and implemented, it must seamlessly integrate with these seven key strategies. There may be other strategies in your toolbox, and others will eventually be added to this list.

As you can see, the concept of continually deploying and integrating new business strategies requires that the leaders use more than traditional, single-issue linear thinking. Leaders must bounce ideas from place to place, allowing the ideas to reflect and glance off one another in a random yet intentional fashion. Most business leaders find this disordered thinking style a bit strange at first. To think in today's complex business environment, however, you must be more creative, use your intuition, and address issues from a multidimensional perspective. Straightforward linear thinking rarely produces innovative ideas. To develop high-level change opportunities, you must learn how to think differently.

The next few paragraphs address the thinking process and provide an understanding of why *unconventional thinking* is necessary and how to do it. The three aspects of unconventional thinking are: creative thinking, multidimensional thinking—which includes system thinking and fuzzy thinking—and intuitive thinking.

CREATIVE THINKING

Creative thinking has never been confined to the poets, artists, and inventors, though the manifestations of their creations usually have a more universal appeal. The product of successful creative thinking is something new in an entirely new context. The newness of the context, however, is the important measure. For example, the Post-it Note was the product of a scientific failure. The scientist was trying to develop a new adhesive. The creative act was in realizing the value of an adhesive that wouldn't permanently adhere and finding a use for it in a totally new context.

Computers can shuffle objects within a context, but they cannot discover new contexts. Humans have this capability because we can and do think out of context— sometimes whether we want to or not. It is that vagary of thought that drives creative thinking. We see things we do not see, hear things we do not hear, and sense things we do not feel. Humans have access to content that extends beyond experiences. The development of new products, systems, and concepts in the outcome management environment requires that leaders understand and apply the concept of creative thinking.

There are three stages of creative thinking, but creativity seldom progresses through these stages in a strict and orderly fashion. Creativity is the fruit born from the tangled vine of conscious and subconscious behaviors.

The first stage is preparation-gathering information. Stage two is the major stage-germination and communication of the creative idea. The third stage is manifestation—giving the idea form and context.

Creative thinking is enhanced when one begins the process with an open mind to reduce the possibility of a conditioned response. It is also important to be persistent in thought to reduce the odds of creating low-probability ideas. Thinking about seemingly unrelated matters also adds value. For example, reading about an unrelated subject often provides a new context for an old thought. Ideas must also be allowed to germinate; the subconscious processing of ideas creates more possibilities than does conscious thinking. The creative act is enhanced by working and talking with others. Involving others increases the probability of a more elegant idea.

Creative Outcome Thinking

Outcome thinking adds a step to the normal process of creative thinking. Typical creative thinking usually begins with a thought that races across the mind. This flash sets the preparation stage—gathering information—in motion. One must consciously and subconsciously search through the databases of the mind for useful information. Stage two—germination and communication—includes reflection on the emerging ideas and the sharing of them with others in the developing state. Stage three gives the ideas life, form, and a context—manifestation. Outcome thinking extends the preparation stage to include a leap to the future. Instead of just examining history, the thinker is encouraged to imagine an outcome as well. Try to decide what you want the future to be like before you come up with the way to get there! This simplified process of creative thinking enhanced with outcome thinking is basically the same process used on a more complex scale by standing teams and project groups when addressing larger issues.

MULTIDIMENSIONAL THINKING

There is an ancient oriental game called GO. The game was invented more than 4,000 years ago in Tibet or China. Today GO has tens of millions of followers all over the world. In Japan, GO is played by more than eight million amateurs and 400 professionals.

The game is played on a 16-inch by 19-inch board marked by 19 horizontal and 19 vertical lines. On the intersections of these lines are placed white or black lens-shaped stones, in the order of each player's turn. Each stone earns its right to stay on the board as long as it can breathe through one of the life lines extending from the point on which it rests to the outside of the board. It may also breathe vertically or horizontally through any adjacent stone of the same color. Players take turns staking out territory—building a protective fortress of stones with an accessible life line and by surrounding, capturing, and thus eliminating the opponent's stones (see Figure 11). The game is won when no further moves are possible. The winner is the player who has captured the most stones and used the greatest number of stones in establishing territories.

The possibilities for strategic development are endless. There are so many possibilities and unpredictable relationships between groups of stones, that it is impossible to cover every one by logical anticipation. Only by seeing the whole picture, with all of its potential, can a player make the moves with the greatest possible impact and meaning. Seeing the whole is the secret to multidimensional thinking. Thoughtless and reflexive moves lead to quick defeat.

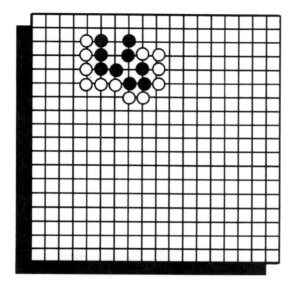

Figure 11. GO

A good GO player is quiet and irrepressible. Beginners tend to see only the trees and overlook the forest. Without a calm mind, a player may dangerously overlook weaknesses.

GO develops a tolerance for ambiguity and incompleteness. Early victories are seductive and can narrow the player's view of the whole board. The game requires intense concentration, but tension upsets the mind and limits perception of potential. GO teaches a person to concentrate on complex and changing situations, under intense competitive pressure, while remaining relaxed enough to make good judgments. An ancient Chinese proverb states: "The moment you think you have understood the problem, your mind begins to grow old." Thinking that you understand a situation is dangerous because it often generates a premature and thoughtless decision. Investing in a lost cause is bad, but missing out on an important opportunity is worse. By looking at the whole board—the system—instead of its individual parts or sections, the potential for opportunity increases and the potential for failure decreases.

In workshops with our clients, we frequently use a version of GO that is played with people on a large electronic game board. The game demonstrates multidimensional thinking in a unique and enjoyable manner.

System Thinking

The ancient oriental game GO is an example of the type of multidimensional thinking required from leaders and managers—system thinking—that is, looking ahead for the implications of each move, instead of just at the immediate effects of them. Dr. Deming often admonished managers for not considering the value of trade-offs when deciding courses of action for their departments or functions. Sometimes it is best for one function to lose strength, if the loss strengthens the whole system. The question to ask is not, "What value can I gain from this proposed action?" but "What value will this action add for the customer and the company (system) as a whole?" Effective system thinking requires the consideration of many issues simultaneously, within the contexts of the effect on the system. Outcome management differs from traditional management philosophies because it is driven by system thinking, not by system analysis.

Fuzzy Thinking

Fuzzy thinking is also a characteristic of multidimensional thinking. It means recognizing the ambiguities of all things and adapting instantly to each new bit of information—shifting and learning as you go. In outcome management, fuzzy thinking means examining the infinite spectrum of options for creating or redesigning a business system, instead of just looking at the one or two most obvious. Allow yourself to think in shades of grey, instead of only in black and white. Let your thoughts glide through one idea into another, never knowing where one ends and another begins—learning as you go.

Out of the interweaving of innumerable ideas, interests, and intentions—be they compatible or opposed—something eventually emerges that has neither been planned nor intended by a single action. Multidimensional thinking provides the texture of surprise to the development of new ideas, contexts, and systems.

Lemonade Begins with Lemons

A small engineering firm in Huntsville, Alabama, had achieved a modicum of success through its minority 8a disadvantaged company status. The company was five years old and recognized as a high performer in designing integrated weapons modeling systems. The success of the company was grounded in the wisdom of its three founders, each representing a minority. The president was knowledgeable in the required technologies, but her primary value to the company was in the area of marketing. The vice-president of operations was just that. He was a master in pushing work through the system, inspiring high-quality performance from his staff and team, and in producing quality deliverables. The third partner was the brains of the company. He was a graduate of a prestigious technology-oriented university and the original sole product of the company. As business increased, however, the work performed by partner number three began to shift to more routine matters. He got caught up in the marketing and in the operations—in the present.

Work in the military and aerospace industry became harder to find as peace began to break out all over the world. 8a disadvantaged companies and others in Huntsville found the pace of competition increasing as defense work diminished. We were asked to help with the redesign of the company's strategic marketing process to more successfully address the changing market demands.

Early in our discussions, we heard partners one and two subtly intimate that partner number three was no longer useful to the company. In fact, it appeared that they thought his leaving would open the door for a staff member who was more in tune with today's technology. Replacing him would create the momentum needed to move into a more productive future. Their struggle with the decision was compounded with their like of and loyalty to partner number three.

We held a secret meeting with partners one and two to discuss their dilemma. Using a force field analysis, we listed the positives and negatives of partner number three and matched each positive with a counter negative. We then suggested that they go back in time and do the same exercise as if they were just starting the company. Because of this exercise and other consultative activities, partners one and two came up with an inventive and creative plan. They decided to focus most of their activities in the present and direct the energies of partner number three to the future. They realized that even if they replaced their partner with the knowledgeable staff person, that move would address only current customer needs—not the future. A primary strength of partner number three was his ability to learn new technologies. They charged him with learning what the company needs to know about the future and with equipping himself to meet it. He has begun taking courses and is being mentored in emerging technologies and programs. He was relieved of all operational duties, and the knowledgeable staff member was elevated to technology expert for the company. Once partner number three acquires sufficient knowledge to become the product again, the three partners will put the newly-elevated staff member in charge of the next future and have him follow a path of re-education similar to that of partner number three. They plan to leap frog these two talented men from future to future. An unconventional answer to the most conventional of all business questions, "How do we get there from here?"

INTUITIVE THINKING

The one rule for successful decision making is: I'll do it if it feels right. Feeling right is a product of intuition. Feeling right about a subject must not be confused with feeling good about it. One can feel right about something without feeling good about it. Feeling right and proceeding forward means having a willingness to take the consequences of your actions because of the rightness of them. Intuition is the ability to gain knowledge or insight without evidence of examination. The key phrase is without evidence of examination. We are the sum of our experiences. Intuitive thinking subconsciously calls on those experiences, but we are also in some strange way more than our experiences.

Though intuitive thinking is grounded in experience, it is more often expressed as a feeling. Experience obviously adds confidence to decision making, but quite often our intuition leads us away from experience toward that which we do not know. Outcome management draws heavily on that which we do not know. In setting a company's vision, modeling ideal systems, and searching for innovations, the successful leader calls on experience, but ultimately relies on feeling in deciding the best course of action. In the case study of the Huntsville engineering company, eliminating partner three didn't feel right. They openly examined options until they created a strategy that did feel right.

UNCONVENTIONAL THINKING

Addressing the complexities and the future focus of outcome management requires unconventional thinking (see Figure 12). The process begins with visioning a desired outcome, then thinking with your conscious mind, your subconscious mind, and your gut. Unconventional thinking is a combination of creative thinking, multidimensional

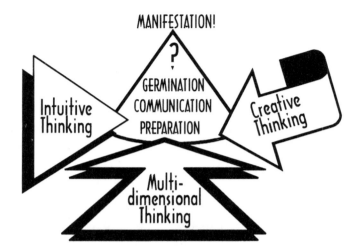

Figure 12. Unconventional Thinking

thinking, and intuitive thinking. It's going to nontraditional sources for inspiration; it's closing your eyes to look
at the big picture, instead of focusing on the facts as they
now appear.

Successful leaders follow the age-old process for creating
something new: They dream before they think, think before
they plan, and plan before they act. Throwing convention to
the wind, they look to the future for new ideas and strategies, process their thoughts through their experiences and
through their subconscious, and then turn to their feelings
for the right action—I'll do it if it feels right.

Thinking unconventionally is key to successful outcome
management. As we explore how to think unconventionally, it is important to remember to always think about the
system as a whole. Keep in mind: Pushing anywhere on the
system causes reactions throughout the entire system.

CHAPTER 8

Putting It All to Work— Integrated Action

"Everything is vague to a degree you do not realize, until you try to make it precise."

—Bertrand Russell

INTERDEPENDENCE

Because of the interdependence of the seven recommended strategies—*technology planning, time reduction, quality discipline, knowledge culture, competitive fitness, activity-based costing, and system redesign*—you can't apply one without addressing them all. In a sense, the strategies are elements of a single self-forming system strategy, because each time an action is taken in or toward one element, the effect is a change in all of them, and throughout the entire system. That constant reformation of strategies in the system provides a powerful force for addressing change.

As you look to the future for challenges to raise your company's performance and profits, each of these strategies, tools, or whatever you wish to call them, must receive attention. One way outcome management differs from other business philosophies is that it demands that each of the strategies be considered in connection and relationship to one another, not just as individual activities. An isolated key system redesign project (reengineering) will probably create more problems than it will solve. Changes to your quality strategy will impact other strategies like cost, technology application, and time reduction. It is important to remember the importance of integrating everything you do. Quality management as a methodology failed most often because it was just attached to the existing management system and never fully absorbed into it.

ERASING THE LINES

The overriding purpose of outcome management is to erase the lines between management, marketing, and operations, creating a whole system focus for planning and work. Those lines were unnecessarily placed there to serve organizational interest, not to serve the interest of the customer. Marketing actions do impact management. A management response affects operations; and around it goes. Outcome management is designed to eliminate departmental, process, and functional thinking and to force everyone to look at the system as a whole. When the entire company is viewed by everyone as an integrated living system, barriers begin to fall, unnecessary work disappears, and the magnitude of achievements increases. The lines between management, marketing, and operations must disappear for any company to advance its potential.

The lines that exist between planning and action must also be removed. In earlier chapters, methodologies for identifying and addressing improvements and creating system redesign breakthroughs were discussed. Outcome management, unlike TQM, focuses these methodologies on results and not on the processes for achieving the results. It is usually a waste of time to break work into little pieces and then try to reconstruct it in a more productive form. It is far more useful to decide on a future and then to determine what kind of work is needed to get the job done.

What difference does it make how thing are done now? Now becomes history before you know it.

LESSONS LEARNED

In the introduction to the book, we identified five basic factors that affect business success—customer wants, the business ecosystem, the company's structure, its business strategies, and its attitude. Customer wants and the business ecosystem (e.g., shifting economic conditions, advancing technologies) are not easily influenced. However, business success depends on leadership's ability to predict those customer wants and the changes to the business ecosystem, and to build a vision drawn from those predictions. That's why outcome management demands that leaders know as much about the customer as does anyone in the company. How else can they predict the future? Business failure invariably comes from attempting to influence the uninfluenceable factors or from ignoring them altogether.

Success also depends on how well leadership addresses challenges through the three influenceable factors: the organization's attitude, its structure, and its strategies. In a growing, productive organization, the attitudes of its people are self-motivating; the structure or principles of the business are self-renewing; and its collection of strategies is self-forming.

Here are the basic elements of attitude, strategies, and structure as we define them:

ATTITUDE	STRATEGIES	STRUCTURE
• Confident leadership	• Quality discipline	• Future aimed
• Collaborative environment	• Knowledge culture	• Mission focused

ATTITUDE	STRATEGIES	STRUCTURE
• Empowered workforce	• Competitive fitness	• Values driven
• Customer focus	• Activity-based costing	• Success factored
• System loyalty	• System redesign	• Measures guided
	• Technology planning	• Synergistic actions
	• Time reduction	

DREAM/THINK/PLAN/ACT

The major difference between outcome management and most other management philosophies is the requirement to vision and think before examining the status of your current situation or past efforts. Instead of beginning with system analysis, outcome management begins with system thinking—visioning the ideal.

Dreaming Up a Vision

First of all, you have to agree that leaning back, placing your feet up on the desk, and closing your eyes is a part of work. Can you imagine walking down the hallway of an allegedly busy concern and seeing office after office of persons daydreaming at their desks? Granted this would be an unconventional sight. But imagine the potential of a work environment in which everyone was encouraged to look ahead, think about the future, and suggest ways of making it better, without fear of condemnation, retribution, or job termination.

Before you adopt the dreaming position, however, you must attend to the preliminaries. Successful dreaming requires that you prepare yourself with knowledge of the future, present, and past. Though ultimately the vision must be drawn from the future, the past and present must be considered. Dreaming up someone else's old idea would probably not prove very useful. The development of a challenging and elevating vision comes from collecting and storing information in the mind and allowing it to ricochet in a random fashion as shown in Figure 13. In this early stage of visioning, nothing is too farfetched and everything is possible.

A client of ours in the distribution business has quadrupled the success of his company with an idea that came to him in a daydream. His company distributes tobacco products to retail outlets. Knowing that this industry is in decline, he began to look for ways to take advantage of the

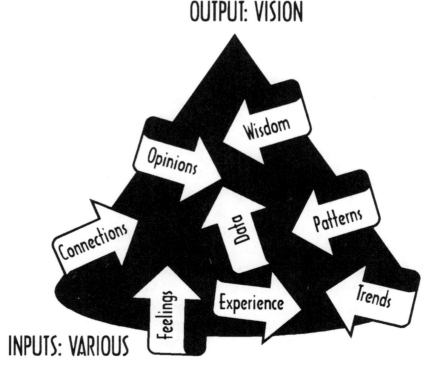

Figure 13. Dreaming

decline instead of falling victim to it. The thought that came to him during a daydream was that his customers were facing the same dilemma as he. Instead of trying to determine how he could save his business, he focused on finding a way he could help save his customers' businesses. His company was already transitioning to gift items and away from reliance on tobacco products. He said to himself, "Why don't we take our knowledge of these changes in the marketplace to our customers?"

Within a few months, the company had developed a software program to manage the inventories of the retail shops that it served. Instead of just selling the retailer a product, the company sold the expertise to transition the retail outlets from a tobacco focus to a gift-shop focus. The company now makes three times more money from selling advice and inventory management than it does from distribution of its products! The idea came to the leader of the business in a daydream.

Thinking Up a Mission

Though dreaming and visioning can be performed by groups, it is basically an individual process. Thinking about business, however, is best done in concert with others. Our definition of business thinking is: conjuring up a mission to address a certain aspect of the company's vision.

In chapter 3, we discussed a study of successful quality management-based companies and identified the key characteristics shared by those companies—*a family view, shared wisdom, collaboration,* and *integrated actions.* In the section on collaboration, we discussed the importance of viewing your co-workers as colleagues when you're involved with them in group thinking. When we learn to think as colleagues, we begin to act as colleagues.

Thinking up a mission is a different process than dreaming up a vision. Visioning is thinking out of context—letting your mind run free. Thinking requires more organization and the consideration of all resources of the company—namely the seven strategies: quality discipline, knowledge culture, competitive fitness, activity-based costing, system redesign, technology planning, and time reduction (see Figure 14). Each of these strategies plays an important role in effective improvement and change. Developing a useful mission requires an examination of the impact of the mission on each single strategy and on their interrelatedness as well.

BIG BANG AT GLAXO

When Glaxo Pharmaceutical began rolling out its quality initiative, the company's leadership chose to go with the

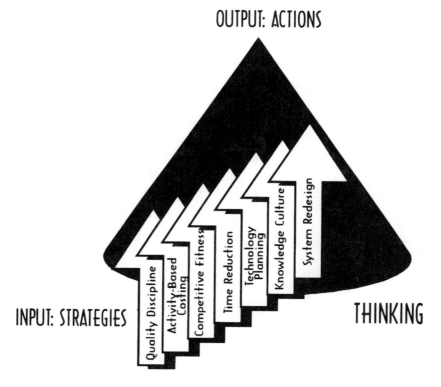

Figure 14. The Seven Strategies of Outcome Management

big bang approach of outcome management. The top leaders of the company first developed a vision that included the following "I want:" to set the performance standards for the rest of the company. Glaxo is the world's second largest pharmaceutical company and is headquartered in London, England. The company has divisions and activities worldwide. To go on record with such a bold declaration required courage, confidence, and risk.

Once the vision was set, assessments were made of the company's management system (quality discipline), the status of its training and education programs (knowledge culture), the competitive environment (competitive fitness), its accounting and costing procedures (activity-based costing), its commitment to change (systems redesign), its information management system (technology planning), and the management of time (time reduction). Glaxo didn't wait, however, until the reports were in to begin its big bang project. Three months before the assessments were to be completed, the company's leadership appointed and empowered a high-level team to address a significant redesign mission.

In the summer of 1993, a mission design retreat was held for one week at the Grove Park Inn meeting facility in Asheville, North Carolina. Using the vision presented by the company's leader, Cliff Disbrow, the 28-member senior planning group gathered to begin to think together in a new and sometimes painful way. Senior members with responsibilities for the seven strategies made presentations to the group on the status of the organization's readiness to move forward.

The big bang project team also made its initial report to the planning group. It was obvious to all the participants that there was no turning back. There was resistance to change during that emotional and highly charged planning session, but there was no denying that change was in the making. After the retreat, thinking together at Glaxo took on a whole new meaning. The senior planning group learned that success in the present and in the future would come from thinking about the system as a whole. No turf or personal territory was excluded from redesign or elimination. No process or function was deemed to be sacred. Everything was now to be considered before any final actions taken. A number of missions related to the vision were developed during the retreat. Several of the missions were designed to upgrade competencies in the seven strategies.

Planning for Action

Once the mission or missions have been determined, it's time to develop a plan for putting them in action. When the mission is clear, the plan will evolve as the planners filter the mission through the structure components—the future, the other missions, measures, values, success factors, and the potential for synchronizing the actions with the other work of the organization's synergistic actions (see Figure 15). Planning may be a group process, a simple collaboration of two or three individuals, or a one-person assignment. The clearer the mission, the simpler the planning process. The senior committee and all other standing plan-

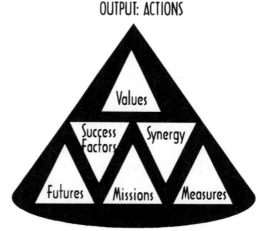

Figure 15.   Planning

ning groups should regularly use these components as a checklist through which to filter each mission they develop.

Strategic planning as it was defined and taught in the past is replete with errors. Even the typical planning cycle that most companies follow often impairs their ability to respond to changes and new challenges. Putting the plan together is often such an exhausting process that if a major business-altering event occurs in the middle of the year, the tendency is to just ignore the event and go forward with the plan as is.

Strategic planning, to be truly effective, must follow strategic visioning. The leaders and mangers in successful companies are comfortable with both visioning and planning.

Planning is no more than developing a set of actions to address the vision and its missions. Visioning means deciding how to behave based on what the future will hold. In planning, you define outcomes or goals, determine actions, commit resources, and aim for defined targets. In visioning, you must ride waves, examine trends, monitor indicators, and predict the future. If you are a leader or manager and visioning sounds uncomfortable to you, you're in the wrong job. Bill Marriott says, "Success is never final." Peter Drucker says, "No matter what the job is, it's never final." Those are great pieces of wisdom to keep in mind when developing or following a plan.

A client, with annual revenues in the billions, operates with a six-page annual plan and a 12-page long-range plan. A supplier to that client, with revenues in the few millions, has an annual plan that is over 100 pages long. The supplier is on notice because of poor performance. Our client asked to see their plan, expecting to hear they had none, based on the problems that had occurred. They were surprised to see a plan of that magnitude. From a review, it became apparent that the last person to read it was the one who wrote it! The practicality of a plan developed with an outcome management philosophy is that it gives you something to change—not that it gives you something to follow come hell or high water.

A mainstay of quality management is the plan-do-check-act (P-D-C-A) cycle (see Figure 16). A change or an improvement is planned. It is then carried out on a small scale. The results are evaluated and then an action is taken. The plan is enacted or it is adapted and run through the cycle again, or it is abandoned because it was found not to add value as expected. The P-D-C-A cycle is the most important tool of process improvement teams in a TQM environment. The eight-step P-D-C-A models used to help explain the dual-track approach follow this basic and fundamental quality management process. The P-D-C-A cycle has proven useful in ensuring that organizations don't adopt a change before determining the potential impact of that change throughout the entire system.

Acting

To keep the planning process stirred up, we recently introduced a new version of the P-D-C-A cycle that begins with act instead of plan and is shown in Figure 17. Several of our

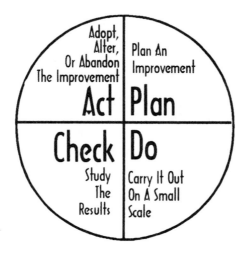

Figure 16. The Plan-Do-Check-Act Cycle

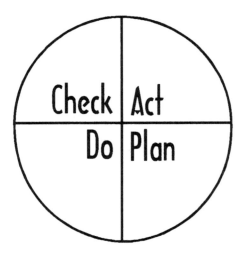

Figure 17.   The Act-Plan-Do-Check Cycle

clients adopted this different way of looking at planning and developed versions of their own. Here are two examples of new planning cycles drawn from the outcome management philosophy:

A-P-D-C cycle. Redesigning a key system might begin with the senior team's acting on instinct, in much the same way that Glaxo's leadership selected its first big bang project. Through instinct, driven by wisdom, the leaders visioned an ideal system and set the process in motion to reach that vision, before determining what the cost would be. The payoff or outcome was deemed to be too important to waste time and money on testing the path to secure it. By establishing a vision and acting upon it, the project team was able to design a workable plan in real time. Through computer modeling and simulation, they were able to create a looks like, acts like, feels like model of their ideal system. Then and only then did they check the outcome by asking themselves the question, "Does this outcome feel right, now that we have experienced it?" The final measure was, "If this feels right, we'll install it!"

Act on instinct; plan from the experience, do a version of the future, check your instincts. This new look at the planning process comes from thinking outside the box, from a willingness to learn new ways of looking at challenges. If you find his process useful, that's great! If you don't, find some other way to do it. The important lesson is that uncommon results come from unconventional approaches.

D-T-P-A cycle. Figure 18 illustrates the dream-think-plan-act cycle. Dream before you think—develop a vision of the future. Think before you plan—create a strategy for achieving the desired outcome. Plan before you act—establish missions for realizing the future. Act—empower everyone with the knowledge, information, tools, and culture needed to succeed.

OUTCOME MANAGEMENT PROCESS

In these two chapters we have pulled together a number of the unconventional themes of outcome management like

Figure 18.   The Dream/Think/Plan/Act Cycle

thinking out of context, planning from the future, and working with ideals instead of existing systems. We've explained why your intuition is a better source of wisdom than is the historical data on the financial statement. In fact we've even told you to learn to think away from the future instead of toward it. We knew when we began to articulate the concept of outcome management that our toughest task would be to transition the reader's thought process from a traditional quantitative approach to an intuitive approach when addressing challenges and opportunities.

Our contention is that the engineering-type of statistical thinking incumbent in TQM discourages the use of intuition and unconventional thinking. The by-the-numbers style of TQM worked well when the goal was incremental improvement. But time is now of the essence. There is no future in the past. And there is no real success to be found in adopting someone else's system. Design your own:

- Create an ideal vision of the future and double-check the organization's attitude.

- Develop a set of precepts like those found in chapter 2 to get your own house in order.

- Simplify and automate all routine work.

- Don't be discouraged when everyone doesn't get it right away.

- Get the structural elements of the business in place—future, missions, value, measures, success factors and synergistic actions.

- Build a strong set of strategies for elevating performance.

- Create missions and key system redesigns without regard for the organization or the resources at hand.

- Empower everyone with the knowledge, information, tools, and culture required to achieve success.

- Get out of the way so good things can happen.

The process just outlined helps identify and remove the
factors that inhibit growth in a company. Learn to identify
and remove the behaviors, steps, and practices that will not
add value to the future you've chosen for your company.

It is very easy, however, to get caught up in the hectic
pace of the present and to ignore the demands of the
future. The future begins with a dream, not with thinking.
Thinking, by definition, is an assessment process. Never
begin planning with an assessment. It limits the scope of
your possibilities. Dreaming is a multilevel, free-style,
eclectic process without parameters.

Reflect on the original dream that set your business life
in motion. Chances are you were in college, working for
someone without a dream, or you had a crazy idea that you
felt just might work. It was at that moment of decision that
you willed your dream into being.

Don't allow yourself to dwell in the past or present.
Look ahead for what you want to happen next.

CHAPTER 9

Technology and Time
Are of the Essence

"Time flows more slowly the farther from the center of the earth."

—Albert Einstein

STRATEGIES

In this chapter, we present technology planning and time reduction. These strategies must be applied in concert with the other five strategies; they are not presented as a menu from which to choose the ones most appealing to you!

TECHNOLOGY PLANNING

Business technology seems to be evolving faster than the business applications for it. When to buy what, for what purpose, and how to separate the fads from the vanguard are recurring dilemmas of leadership. Businesses, on the other hand, are often more capable of evolution and change than their leaders are in finding and deploying advanced technological tools.

Information and employed technology are shifting from the development phase into the application phase.

Though technology will continue to change, the advances will be more in the arena of application than in the development of altogether new technologies.

During this shift from technology's development to application phase, it is especially important for a company to have an intentional technology planning process that is both flexible and forward thinking. The last thing a company would want to do is to retool its technology just to meet current needs. Technology planning must be focused on what the business is becoming, not what it is.

Information Infrastructure and Role

Technology, particularly information technology, in the business setting can be viewed as the path and the energy that makes up the company's infrastructure, similar to the roads, sewer lines, electricity, and gas connections found in a residential development. Like the real estate developer's infrastructure planning, technology planning must address future demands on the system, as well as current needs.

Information drives business. Technology generates, processes, stores, and transmits information. Generating information means preparing information to be sent in a form that is easily understood by the receiver. The computer made its first contribution in processing information—starting with data processing, then word processing, and on to voice and image processing. Data, word, voice, and image are the four basic forms of information.

Storing means taking one of the four information forms and keeping it for later use. Computer storage is a more dynamic process than paper storage because the technology allows you to retrieve and change as well as hold. *Transmitting* means sending and receiving all forms of information. Whereas computers generate, process, and store information, telecommunications is the primary mode of transmission.

Follow or Lead?

A difficult task of leading a business is deciding how and when to apply new technologies—automation and telecommunications. When a firm leads, it is betting on an unproven and maybe unstable technology—risky business. When it follows, it is betting that it can catch up to its competition without suffering loss—also risky business. We suggest there is a better question to be asking than, "Follow or lead?" It is, "What kind of technology do we need to address the challenges we have chosen to face?"

When looking for the answer to that question, you must be honest with yourself. Don't be fooled into thinking you're addressing future needs, when you're only playing catch-up. Here are four measures for determining the value of a particular technology to the present or future of the company:

- *Operational necessity*—We have to do this just to remain efficient and responsive.

- *Competitive necessity*—We have to do this or fall behind our competition in terms of product, price, or service.

- *Improvement necessity*—Doing this now will push us ahead of our competitor in product, price, or service.

- *Breakthrough necessity*—Doing this now will substantially change the dynamics of the business we are in and make us the recognized leader.

Operational, competitive, and improvement necessities are present focused and, though necessary, risky propositions when addressed alone. If your technology planning process focuses only on updating and incrementally improving existing processes, even success can put you out of business. Technology planning must be driven by a vision of the desired future (i.e., a breakthrough necessity). Putting in an infrastructure that meets only short-term and mid-term needs will ultimately lead to failure.

The Paperless Promise

With the advent of the business computer in the late 1960s came the prediction of the paperless office. In the past decade, the technocrats promised performance improvements in direct proportion to the application of advancing technologies. But in today's business environment the amount of paper used is up tenfold, and the billions spent on business automation has not delivered a proportional value of increased performance.

For many, a heavy investment in technology has produced disappointing results—largely because automation was used to mechanize the old ways of doing business instead of to find new ways. The lesson learned is that speed does not address performance deficiencies. More often than not, speed expands the impact of the deficiencies and creates an additional barrier to improved performance.

Outcome management as a methodology relies heavily on technology as it looks to the future for answers. Imaging ideal systems and modeling and testing a wide array of options are often greatly enhanced by technology. Each year new modeling and visioning tools are introduced into the system thinking and system redesign processes.

Most of the problems of underperforming systems stem from business leaders' either ignoring, not recognizing, or underestimating the shift from the seller's to buyer's market and the speed required for creating and moving new products in today's marketplace. Technology planning, therefore, is often relegated by those leaders to automating existing systems and improving the flow of information throughout the organization.

Thinking/Planning/Redesigning

Besides generating, processing, storing, and transmitting information, technologies can provide a glimpse into the future. Computer simulations, such as those developed to predict the performance of rockets and missiles, can now simulate a manufacturing process and predict the output of a production line before it is built or modified, thus saving millions of dollars.

For example, a manufacturing process is a set of inter-related elements that produce an output by using input from the business environment. A manufacturing process includes labor, materials, management direction, customer research, and financial resources as input. This input is then transformed into an output or finished product. To redesign this process and make it more responsive to cus-tomer demand requires consideration of the system as a whole. Attitudes, the vision, other processes, missions, and certain external factors will all impact and be impacted by the change. All of these elements must be built into the sim-ulation process. The steps for developing an effective sim-ulation are to:

- Set a mission by visioning an ideal system.
- Establish a desired outcome and collect the pertinent data.
- Validate the model through intuition and the struc-ture components.
- Run the simulations and analyze the results.
- If it feels right, install it!

Empowerment Through Technology

Empowerment is leadership's providing the knowledge information, tools, and culture with which everyone can perform and improve work—in accordance with the company's vision and missions. Knowledge and information are power. In a traditional hierarchical organization, knowledge was usually reserved for those at the top, information was passed down on a need-to-know basis, and tools were usually selected and distributed by managers.

In the collaborative environment of outcome management, knowledge is shared and created throughout the system, all information is available to everyone, and tools are often selected or even designed by those who use them. Advancing technologies have increased the availability of information, expanded the quest for knowledge, and reduced the cost of making information available to everyone.

It is through the aggressive and diligent collection and dissemination of information that smart decisions are made, on which superior performance is built, and from which visions become reality.

Technology planning has become a senior-level responsibility and an important strategy to business success. New and emerging technologies are no longer used solely to collect and share information, but also to aid in decision making and to advance the search for new ideas, products, services, and profits.

In fact, many of the complex data manipulation tasks that were necessary to deploy a quality management system in years past have become routine with advanced software programs. Process mapping, for example, is now a data-in, information-out process. Numerous software programs are available to facilitate process mapping. These days, no one would consider drawing a flow chart by hand or collecting statistical data on a yellow pad.

Modeling and simulation programs expand the dreaming and what-if processes. The concept of key system redesign was considerably more difficult in the early dual-track deployment days without today's sophisticated programs. It is important for any company, large or small, to know about the array of technology and technological resources available to make work easier or to eliminate it altogether. But it is more important to have a strategy to deploy these advances in a manner that adds appropriate value for the customer and the company in a timely and profitable fashion.

In an outcome management environment, technology is used to ensure that everyone has the knowledge, information, and tools required to perform and improve work.

TIME REDUCTION STRATEGY

Stanley Davis, in his book *Future Perfect*, suggests that time has become the most valuable raw material of commerce. How we use our time, concludes Davis, has become the primary measure of success in both our business and personal lives. In the workplace, those who find ways to increase the availability of time have a decided advantage. One of the primary benefits of quality management is the promise of eliminating the need for rework through the continuous improvement process. The premise is that time spent in getting better will generate more time for thinking and planning and that increased thinking and planning time will ultimately lead to better products, service, and marketing, which will lead to increased profitability.

Whereas the goal of management is to find more time to address additional challenges, problems, and opportunities, in marketing the goal is to reduce the time between identifying and satisfying the customer's need. Reduce the time between concept and consumption, and value is added to the product or service. The provider that can deliver the same product at the same price in 20 percent less time will win the race and the customer.

In the manufacture of products the concept of just-in-time (JIT) inventory has received great attention over the past decade. The way to detect what is holding back production is to reduce inventories or stock levels enough to expose operating deficiencies that are normally masked by buffers of stockpiled parts. Once the operating deficiencies are identified, a process is developed to have parts produced and received just when they are needed, thereby eliminating the need for buffers and the cost of holding and storing unneeded inventories.

By now most companies realize the need for an ongoing time reduction strategy. The driver of a time reduction strategy is cost. Time is money. Business leaders are more likely to adopt and support the time reduction strategy than they are the six other strategies because its stated objective is to eliminate cost.

One of the earliest proponents of a time reduction strategy was the Swiss manufacturing conglomerate Asea Brown Boveri (ABB). In fact their management philosophy is expressed as total quality time-based management.

ABB Kent-Taylor

The ABB Kent-Taylor plant in Rochester, New York, assembles power transformer metering devices. Though ABB is highly recognized around the world for its quality/time-based management successes, the plant in Rochester was recently acquired and new to the ABB management philosophy.

Their introduction to the corporate quality emphasis began with a customer assessment conducted by the Boston Consulting Group. The study indicated that delivery time was the most important factor to the customer, and that the competition, for the most part, had a delivery schedule similar to that of the ABB subsidiary. The Kent-Taylor plant was operating on a delivery cycle of 6 to 12 weeks. The customers for the metering devices, however, wanted a three-week turnaround. If the company could meet the customer's needs, it would provide a significant competitive advantage.

We were engaged to lead the delivery system redesign project and to assist the company with the deployment of the other aspects of the parent company's quality/time-based management process. The redesign team was led by Chris Bigalow of Kent-Taylor and included four staff engineers and two consultants from our group. The mission was to reduce assembly time from three months to two weeks maximum. From a comprehensive root cause analysis we found redundant testing, leakages and pressure problems in welding and soldering processes, and buffering of components that led to uneven assembly flows and the masking of other defects and problems.

Through the process of modeling a number of possible solutions—drawn from current knowledge, competitive intelligence, and evaluations of new technologies—we were able to redesign the assembly portion of the product delivery system to a procedure that took only four days from start to finish. A two-day cycle was possible if an alternative could be found to replace an epoxy resin used in the assembly process that required a 24-hour drying time.

The redesign focused on the assembly process, not on product improvement. The factory floor space required for the procedure was reduced by 50 percent and the company was able to add five more production lines, and there was a one-time savings from the redesign in excess of $6 million. ABB Kent-Taylor also entered into a joint venture with the manufacturer of the epoxy resin to develop a product with a faster drying time.

Time-Based Competition

Customers will pay for time. Develop a reputation for delivering products and services ahead of expectation and your customer base will expand. *Information Management* reported that, on the average, high-tech products that come to market six months late but on budget will earn 33 percent less profit over a five-year life cycle.

Hewlett-Packard CEO John Young says, "Doing it fast forces you to do it right the first time." If you don't build-in time for correcting mistakes, more effort will be put into integrating the design function with the product production system, thereby eliminating mistakes in the first place and reducing the time between concept and consumption.

FEWER ARROWS MORE BULL'S EYES

The master archer saw the student facing the target holding two arrows. "Beginners shouldn't hold two arrows," admonished the teacher. "Counting on the second arrow results in carelessness with the first. Each time, determine that you will settle the matter with one arrow. Do not worry about whether or not you will succeed."

"With only two arrows and in the presence of the teacher," asked the student, "would one really be careless with an arrow?"

"You may not be aware of any slackening, but I will know," answered the master archer. "When someone practices an art, he always thinks he has another chance, so is not aware of slackness. Slackness is very difficult to perceive in the immediacy of the moment."

CHAPTER 10

Quality and Knowledge—
Roots and Wings

"He who has imagination without learning has wings but no feet."

—Fortune Cookie

STRATEGIES

This chapter discusses two of the seven strategies for successful outcome management: quality discipline and a knowledge culture.

QUALITY DISCIPLINE

A quality discipline has become a business imperative, while terms like *total quality management, quality improvement,* and even the word *quality* have taken on negative connotations. At one time it was quite vogue to engage in quality talk. The quality movement created more buzzwords than all the other management paradigms combined. But nowadays, quality talk raises eyebrows and loses the attention of audiences at workshops, seminars, and speaking engagements.

Boise Cascade has derived great success from its five-year-old TQM initiative. The organization's quality steering committee is now working, however, to remove all mention of TQM's buzzwords from its vision, mission, and goal statements. "Our quality system," says Boise quality director Jim Peterson, "has become the way we do business period. We want all statements about ourselves to reflect this evolution." Boise is in no way denying its commitment to its quality discipline. They've just realized it's time to recognize the maturing of Boise's quality initiative, to reflect the demands of the times, and to take advantage of the lessons learned from the quality process. We have always recommended that companies not name their management philosophy. When a company adopts TQM, outcome management, or any other new philosophy and gives it a name, the effort is often viewed as an additional layer of work, not a new way of doing things. Some companies do identify their management philosophies, with success. But the best way to proceed is to create the feeling that "this is not only the new way, but the only way we perform our duties around here."

Quality is in the eye of the beholder and the customer is that beholder in the world of commerce. The quest for quality is grounded in awareness of the current needs and future demands of the customer. Business success depends on the company's meeting those needs and demands faster, better, and at a lower cost than does the competition. An effective quality discipline focuses on the customer, is centered in collaborative work, built on the continuous improvement of that work, and driven by a clear and challenging vision from the company's leaders.

Focus on the Customer

We have shifted our view of a company from that of a single entity to that of a system that operates within a larger system of living dynamic relationships—a global business ecosystem.

Of the five basic factors that affect business success—the business ecosystem, the company's operating structure, the foundation of the business, the attitude of those connected with the business, and customer wants—we deal primarily with the three factors which can be directly influenced by the leaders of the company—foundation, structure, and attitude. The customer and the business ecosystem that surrounds the company are not easily influenced.

When technology changed the world of commerce from the seller's to buyer's market, the role of the customer was elevated to monarch status. The customer may even be viewed as the head of the corporate family and placed in a block on the organizational chart ahead of the chairman of the board. The customer's responsibility as a member of the corporate family is to define the quality of the organization's output.

The customer has also been more inclusively defined as any user of an output of a company, a system, a process, or even an individual. The concept of viewing others in the workplace as internal customers was made popular by the quality movement. It is a valuable proposition from which to define and value work.

It is in the marketplace, however, that the customer is king. The purpose of using a quality discipline as a strategy is to ensure that everyone knows what it's going to take to get the customer to brag about the company's products and services and that they use that understanding to perform and improve work accordingly.

Centered in Collaboration

Smart companies have learned that people work better in collaboration than in layers. Providing an environment that fosters collaboration is a primary imperative of man-

agement. Collaboration includes working together and
working independently toward a common cause. It also
includes working in teams to improve and redesign work.
The successful work of teams depends on:

- A clear mission.
- Customer knowledge.
- A system view.
- Established ground rules.
- Diversity of opinion.
- Ongoing communication.
- Education to the tasks.
- Reward and recognition.

It is important that the development stages of any team
or group be understood, particularly if you are the primary
source of that group's empowerment. When joining a
group, an individual experiences three basic concerns:

- **Inclusion**—"Who else is here and how far can I trust
  them?"
- **Control**—"Who's calling the shots? What will be
  required of me? Can we say what we think without
  hurting or getting hurt?"
- **Affection**—"What if I don't get along with some of
  these people? Can we show our true feelings for one
  another and still achieve our mission?"

The leader of a group must be aware of this process and
address these concerns early in the group's formation.
Many teams go forward with individuals still wrestling
with these issues and therefore unable to make the quality
of contributions expected from them. That is a process failure, not the fault of the individual.

The purpose of collaboration is to create change, but even change for the better is a stressor. The coping process is a behavioral response to stress. Coping begins with denial, creates anxiety, and leads often to anger and guilt, to depression, and finally moves the person or the group to a new steady state. The leader and group's awareness of the coping process reduces the cycle time required for the process to run its course. Understanding group dynamics and group psychology is fundamental to leading a successful company.

And as emphasized in earlier chapters, high-level collaboration, like that required for an effective quality discipline, is possible only in an organizational environment with a reward system based on people working together.

Built on Improvement

The process of continuous improvement is that of the organization track of the dual-track approach presented in chapter 4. It is up to the senior team to establish a system improvement plan from which improvement missions are assigned or developed by standing improvement teams. This aspect of a quality discipline is the basis of traditional TQM or quality management. Outcome management extends the ongoing process to include system redesign as well. It is on this organization track, however, that routine work is improved and where the team activities provide knowledge and experience for those who will serve on the more complex system redesign teams.

Driven by Vision

Outcome management is a journey that is driven by a vision. The journey begins with an awareness of the destination or the purpose for the journey. Every company's journey is different because of the opportunities, obstacles, and challenges it meets along the way and because of the uniqueness of its personality and resources. The leader establishes the destination and the purpose for the journey. An effective quality discipline is driven by the vision of the leader.

Read No Further

If the description of the quality discipline is not in sync with the activities in your company, read no further. This focused attention to quality as defined by the customer and arrangement of work to successfully address the demands of the customer should be a given by now in any commercial setting. Of the seven strategies we present, the maintenance of a quality discipline is the only absolute. Without it, there is no future in the future or anywhere else. You might as well just close up shop right now.

KNOWLEDGE CULTURE

What is work? Work is the process of meeting the customer's and the company's needs. An important characteristic of work that is often overlooked is the process of acquiring knowledge. Successful companies include the acquisition of knowledge as a part of their definition of work. Maintaining a knowledge culture means the inclusion of education along with the company's regular training program. Education is different from training. Education means giving everyone the opportunity to elevate abilities and talents to meet the future demands of the business. Training is the process of providing people with the tools they need to get the most out of the tasks they are currently performing.

Leaders Need Education

The enormity of information, the hectic pace of business, and the variety of challenges faced by senior executives make it difficult for them to include education as a part of their work. But these very factors that draw the busy executive away from education demand that education be an integral part of work.

To supplement their continuing education, many successful leaders rely on outside mentors and consultants and join executive discussion groups. The busy executive can't always find time to read the latest book, to study for a week at the local university, or to objectively evaluate all the options, ideas, and challenges of running the business. By using a mentor who has an understanding of the specific challenges of the company as well as a grasp of current business knowledge, the leader can condense the time required to gather new wisdom for decision making.

Having a mentor or an objective colleague is a necessity in today's business environment. There are issues and decisions that must be objectively discussed in a context outside the organizational structure. Chambers of commerce throughout the country have established effective low-cost programs that provide business leaders with opportunities to work with mentors and colleagues to develop their leadership and management skills. There are several for-profit companies that provide similar services. The American Management Association conducts myriad programs for leaders at its education facility at Saranac Lake, New York, and throughout the nation.

There are many experienced and knowledgeable consultants who could serve as coaches to leaders and managers. But most consultants don't take their own medicine, and they continue to focus on the training and problem-solving aspects of their work. They find it uncomfortable to look for new ways to better serve their clients, so they continue to sell what they do, instead of what they know. They don't realize that the most useful advice is sometimes given away at the water cooler or over dinner.

Education for Everyone!

Continuing education for everyone else is as important as it is for the leaders. If the vision of the future is as full of promise as it should be, doesn't it make sense that all the brainpower in the company be commissioned and sharpened to meet the challenge? Employees should be encouraged to take courses at local universities and trade schools that will be paid for by the employer. Encouraging education and rewarding it as a part of work is sometimes a difficult concept for CEOs to understand because the payoff appears to be long term. It does, however, have a short-term benefit as well. The employee feels respected, trusted, included, and valued when allowed to improve on his or her own terms. Recognizing education as a part of work elevates performance and productivity and creates a healthy work environment.

Training

Have you ever sat through a training session and wondered, "Why are we wasting all this time?" One of the biggest criticisms of TQM is that the training in the tools and processes is often ineffective and usually mistimed. When the training program doesn't meet the needs of the company, it is because the company's leaders haven't taken the time to understand it. More often than not, leaders approve training budgets and programs without a clue as to their role or value.

Most companies have established in-house training programs. In manufacturing, these programs are often staffed by engineers right off the shop floor. In service areas, the trainers usually come from a public relations or human resources background. Though these persons may be highly skilled in their areas of expertise and talented in communicating information to others, their training programs are often weak and ineffective. They are rarely given any training themselves in curriculum design, the psychology of learning, or other subjects that might prove helpful. Often they rely on the only related experience they have—that of being a student. Their curriculum, therefore, follows the typical classroom style they are accustomed to.

A company recently moved into a new building. As a part of the move, there was some shuffling of personnel. A very competent stenographer was elevated to receptionist. The requirements of the receptionist were complex and numerous. The young woman who received the promotion was bright and energetic. She had been with the company for three years and was well known and liked by all. Concurrent to the move a new telephone system was installed. A representative from the phone company trained the receptionist and the office manager in its use.

After about two weeks, it became painfully obvious that the young woman was not emotionally suited or skilled for the hectic and dynamic pace required to manage the foot traffic and the phones. Clients and employees were complaining, and the regard for this once-valued employee was diminishing. The senior staff empowered the office manager to move the receptionist back to the stenographer position at her elevated salary and to hire a new receptionist as soon as possible. About a week later we arrived at the company for an early-morning meeting, where we witnessed the unsuccessful receptionist training her replacement!

So we have the unsuccessful training their successors, and the untrained training others, and the company's leaders approving budgets and training curricula. Sound like your company?

What's wrong with training? Nobody takes the time to learn how to do it, including many of those who are considered to be training professionals. The biggest problem, however, is that leaders and managers don't take the time to understand what training can and cannot do, or when and how it works best. Knowledgeable educators will tell you that the lecture is the least effective way to educate and train adults. Yet we find that most corporate training programs are lecture based. One reason for this is economics. It is less costly for a staff trainer in a large company to develop a lesson plan, overheads, and a narrative presentation of a subject matter, than it is to bring in a subject-matter expert to mentor those who need to be trained. And most companies require the training department to submit a budget for the annual training program, when neither the trainers nor the leadership have a clue as to what training may be needed. The training department is then required to provide all the necessary training and stay within the budget. In fact, they are rewarded if they come in under budget. In a company you can always expect the type of behavior that you reward. Trainers who are rewarded for saving money will develop programs based on cost, and not on results. In small companies, the leader will often default the training decision to an untrained administrative assistant or to the person who needs the training. Leaders of companies of all sizes must become familiar with when, how, and what to train on more than a superficial level.

Teaching Versus Learning

It is important for those who approve training and education budgets and courses to understand what they are approving and have some guarantee that the dollars allocated will be well spent. The foundation of knowing education's value when you see it is in understanding the difference between teaching and learning.

The primary function of any education system is to release the ability to gain understanding on one's own. The curriculum should be designed to develop understanding, provide new knowledge and information, and create wisdom. Information and knowledge enable us to increase efficiency. Wisdom enables us to improve effectiveness.

What we know is what we have learned, but not necessarily what we have been taught. Most education and training systems are designed for teaching, not for learning.

There are four basic problems with most training and teaching systems:

1. The teacher emphasizes transmitting rather than receiving. We actually learn more by talking than by listening. Talking gives us the opportunity to discover what we do not know. Students should be encouraged to articulate their understanding.

2. The teacher assumes that the student is ignorant. Many managers assume that they know more about the work of their subordinates than their subordinates know. The same is often true of teachers. Many teaching systems in corporate settings underestimate the intelligence and understanding of the student and, therefore, waste time and money teaching people things they already know.

3. The teacher discourages creativity. An instructor's desire to stay with the prepared lesson plan and to constrain discussion and feedback limits the student's potential for creative input. It encourages conformity, rather than diversity. There is no creative force in conformity.

4. The teacher uses tests to measure learning. Most tests measure what was memorized, not what was learned. How much students learn depends more on their ability to learn and on the opportunities for learning than on the instruction. Tests should provide an additional opportunity for learning, but they seldom do.

Learning Versus Teaching

Good teachers and trainers are more than disseminators of information. They must know how to instill learning and how to develop knowledge in their students. People must have a balance of technical expertise and appreciation for the tasks they are to perform. Good training includes the whys and the wherefores along with the hows.

Encouraging people to think raises the entire organization to higher levels of proficiency. The most powerful learning comes from experience, through taking action and seeing the consequences of that action, then taking a new or different action. A successful learning system provides hands-on experience. For example:

- Some subjects are best learned by teaching them to others.

- Some subjects are best learned by teaching them to oneself.

- Some skills are best learned through demonstration and instruction by one who already has the skill.

- Seminars are effective when led by someone expert in the subject matter and when the subject is one already familiar to the student.

- Many students learn best under real-life situations by solving real problems.

- Lectures may be useful, if the lecturer has the ability to stimulate and hold the students' attention; subject-matter knowledge is secondary.

Most training directors with any experience at all know that different subjects are best taught in different ways, that adults learn differently from children, and that individuals learn in ways different from their peers. Yet the training directors continue to search for the familiar simple-to-use, cheap-to-buy, off-the-shelf stuff to stay within the budget. They take the safest course of action instead of searching for the best. Taking the safe course is an indication that empowerment from the top is incomplete and that collaboration is not yet the primary measure of reward.

The Natural Learning Process

Several years ago we introduced a curriculum development process to our clients based on the work of Richard

Bandler and John Grinder in neuro-linguistic programming. The U.S. Army's Organizational Effectiveness School uses a similar process it calls new patterns of influence. Dr. Seymour Johns, author of *The New Psychology of Personal Excellence,* is also an expert in the sensory-based learning system.

Our system of learning is called the natural learning process (NLP). NLP begins with the premise that learning is a process acquired through the use of one or more of the five senses: sight, sound, touch, taste, and smell. In each learner, one of these senses is dominant. Through the use of the natural learning process evaluation instrument, the teacher designs a curriculum to appeal to each student's dominant sense. The teacher adjusts to the needs of the student, rather than forcing the student into the teacher's mold. We have used NLP to assist companies with the development of their knowledge cultures. The responsibility for carrying out a company's knowledge culture strategy is usually housed in the company's business school, training programs, continuing education process, or human resources department. It is the leader's responsibility, however, to see that the appropriate learning occurs, no matter where the company's learning program is carried out. Small companies should contract with area business schools and colleges to provide learning opportunities that are beyond the scope of the company's internal capabilities.

We've found that learning is more effective when based on sensing. Our learning system is based also on the premise that anything learned through more than one sense will be better learned and longer remembered. The old adage claims, "We remember 10 percent of what we see, 20 percent of what we hear, and 30 percent of what we see and hear." The NLP approach expands that concept to include experiencing as well.

For example, a person who is visual learns best from a teacher who uses diagrams, charts, and pictures to illustrate the subject being taught. If the instructor uses only oral explanations, the visual person may have trouble absorbing the new information, no matter how exact the instructions are and no matter how patient the teacher is. With a visually dominant student the teacher should use visual terms like, "What do you see on the screen?" Auditory learners require verbal explanations like, "The lesson says what to you?" Individuals who learn best through their feelings (intuition) find it helpful to imagine they are performing the procedure. The teacher might say, "What do you think you should do next?"

The bottom line of the natural learning process is that the teacher must be aware of the dominant sense of each student and be able to adjust the presentation of the subject matter to the learning style of the student.

The biggest problem in using the NLP model for curriculum design is almost always the training director. Because leaders don't often understand the psychology of learning and have very little knowledge from which to approve budgets, training directors are forced into the traditional and the familiar when developing training and education programs. They develop that which the boss will approve, not that which will best serve the demands of the customer and the company.

The research of Bandler and Grinder suggests that the greatest obstacle to learning a new technique or procedure is the emotional limits that the individuals place on themselves. With NLP the emotions become part of the learning process. Through the inclusion of visceral experiences, the learned potential for internalizing the new knowledge is increased. The individual therefore becomes more comfortable and confident at a faster pace. This, coupled with the transformation of hard data, accelerates learning and makes it more meaningful.

Leaders Must Lead

Creating and maintaining a knowledge culture is one of the most important jobs of a business leader. Knowledge acquisition must be celebrated as a part of work. It is up to the leader to set the standards for continuous learning and to set the example.

The leader should provide a clear understanding of what is expected from the company's training and education programs. The leader's participation in the process validates it and helps the leader understand the hows, the whys, and the payoff of the programs. The graph presented in Figure 19 is an example of a training and education program based on the theories presented here and in the natural learning process.

Quality and Knowledge

In this chapter we have discussed two of the seven strategies that are basic to the leader's toolbox, through which all new ideas for redesign and improvement must be filtered,

CORE CURRICULUM	Lecture/Seminar	Audio/Visual	Computer-Aided	Work Project	Self-Study	Study Teams	LEADERS	MANAGERS	STAFF	LINE	CUSTOMER/SUPPLIER
Understanding the Vision	✓	✓					●	●	●	●	
Focus on the Customer	✓	✓		✓	✓		●	●	●	●	●
Working in Teams		✓		✓		✓	●	●	●	●	●
Aiming at Quality	✓	✓	✓	✓	✓	✓	●	●	●	●	●
Using Information	✓	✓	✓		✓	✓	●	●	●		●
Cycle Time Compression	✓	✓	✓			✓	●	●	●		
Redesigning Systems	✓	✓	✓				●	●	●		
Improving Processes	✓		✓				●	●	●		
Planning Your Work	✓	✓		✓			●	●	●	●	
Leading Teams	✓	✓		✓			●	●	●		
Personal Growth	✓	✓		✓	✓		●	●	●		
Group Process	✓	✓		✓			●	●	●		
Unconventional Thinking	✓	✓		✓	✓	✓	●	●	●		
Managing Outcomes	✓			✓	✓		●	●	●		
Computer Skills			✓	✓	✓		●	●	●		
Grammar and Writing	✓		✓		✓		●	●	●	●	
General Math	✓		✓		✓		●	●	●	●	
Business Communication	✓		✓		✓		●	●	●	●	

Figure 19. Sample Training and Education Program

and that provide the foundation for a successful outcome management environment.

The quality discipline has become a *given*. Without a focus on the customer, a center in collaboration, continuous improvement of work, and a vision from the leader, a company doesn't stand a chance.

A knowledge culture demands that the quest for knowledge become an integral part of work. The company must provide training to meet today's needs and education to meet tomorrow's demands. Outcome management draws on knowledge past, present, and future, and requires a commitment to learning something new every day.

CHAPTER 11

Fitness and Facts—Winning Through Preparation

"Knowledge of his own conditions but not the conditions of the enemy has an even chance of winning and losing a battle. He who has neither a thorough knowledge of his own conditions nor of the enemy's is sure to lose every battle."

—Sun Tzu

WHO IS THE ENEMY?

MedParts, Inc. is a remanufacturer and remarketer of CAT scan equipment. Several years ago when General Electric decided to get out of the CAT-scan business, the principals of MedParts were able to purchase G.E.'s entire 8800 and 9800 CAT-scan parts and components inventory at scrap prices. There are more than 8,000 8800 and 9800 CAT scans in service throughout the world.

We assisted them with the total redesign of the company's equipment stream process and its marketing system. The traditional process for acquiring equipment for remanufacture was through an informal user network. As a marketing strategy, MedParts also sold parts and serviced the CAT scans of current owners. The company also maintained relationships with individuals who brokered sales, and responded to used-equipment advertisements that appeared in two or three medical technical journals. Most opportunities, however, usually came in over the phone from hospitals with used equipment for sale or from the independent brokers.

Independent brokers and companies that leased CAT scan equipment were the company's primary competitors. These leasing companies had a decided advantage because of the stream of used equipment available from the leasing arrangements. Every remanufacture by MedParts required a financial investment in a used CAT scan. The competition already owned the used machine when it came off lease— an additional competitive advantage.

When MedParts entered the marketplace, a new CAT scan sold for more than $1,000,000. They could sell a refurbished version for about $200,000. Within two years, however, a dramatic event occurred.

Several Japanese companies decided to become serious contenders for new CAT scan sales. In typical Japanese fashion, their long-range marketing strategy was to capture the entire market by setting prices below U.S. manufacturing costs, thus putting the American manufacturers out of business. Prices on new CAT scans began to fall rapidly, thereby driving down used equipment sales and creating additional competition for MedParts.

We initiated an extensive intelligence gathering program from which we discovered three seemingly unconnected pieces of valuable information. First, the sellers of new equipment usually took the old CAT scans in on trade. They usually sold the used CAT scan to one of the independent brokers, who then sold it to MedParts or someone else. Second, the new-equipment seller got paid when the new CAT scan became operative. Installation, however, depended on how quickly the independent could get the old CAT scan sold, disassembled, and out of the way. Third, MedParts was the only company in the industry with its own truck line.

When these three seemingly unrelated pieces of information were put together, an innovative and unconventional idea emerged. Why not develop a relationship with the new-equipment manufacturers to purchase all of their trade-ins and guarantee to remove the old CAT scan within 36 hours of notification? And in exchange get them to agree to a 90-day delay in receiving payment for the old equipment. This arrangement, when implemented, gave Medparts a used-equipment stream equal to or better than its leasing competitors, eliminated the company's up-front cost, and solved a major logistics and revenue problem for the sellers of new equipment.

COMPETITIVE FITNESS PROGRAM

The story of Medparts is a success story of positioning, strategy, and competition. All business wins are not as bloodless as this one. Competition is fierce. To compete, one must be prepared not only physically for the fight but mentally as well. Mental preparedness means knowing the strengths and weaknesses of your opponents as well as your own competencies and vulnerabilities. A competitive fitness program includes continuous study of the marketplace and the competition as well as a process for identifying the company's core competencies.

There is a difference between intelligence gathering and benchmarking. Intelligence gathering is collecting information from a variety of sources from which smart decisions can be made. Intelligence gathering is an important part of a successful benchmarking process. Benchmarking is a process for examining business practices of others and determining whether adopting or adapting those practices within the processes of the examining company would be worthwhile.

The American Society for Industrial Security reported in 1993 that industrial espionage had increased 260 percent since 1985. The primary targets of these illegal activities are technology, trade secrets, and business plans. What if you knew exactly what your major competition had up their sleeves? Would it make that much difference in your decision making? Or more important, if your competition knew what you were up to, would it make any difference to them?

There are many legitimate means for gathering competitive data. In fact there is so much useful information just sitting around in databases gathering particles, one has to wonder why all the illegal activity. Getting stung by a competitor's action usually comes not from a lack of warning, but from an absence of an early warning system. An effective competitive fitness program identifies traditional and nontraditional competition and tracks their activities. A traditional competitor is one within the same basic industry: Kimball, Yamaha, and Steinway make pianos. A nontraditional competitor is one that competes for the same dollar. Javelin makes boats. Boats and pianos often compete for the same dollar. More often, the decision as to how to spend disposable dollars comes down to buying the boat or the piano, not which boat or piano to buy.

Intelligence Gathering

Though trade journals and regional newspapers rarely tell the whole story, you can often piece several stories together to get an accurate picture of what your competition is planning to do.

We once received a call inviting us to meet with members of the management team at Glaxo Pharmaceuticals to discuss the possibility of our involvement in their new management philosophy initiative. During the conversation we accessed CompuServe through the computer modem, typed in "Glaxo," and within five minutes, before the conversation was completed, we had in-hand three of 14 available articles on the company at a cost of $4.50! Granted, the information we received was not high-level secret information on the company's activities. But the story is an example of how simple it is to access online business information databases from your office or home.

The second best source of information is most often your own company's sales staff and customers. You'd be surprised at what they know if you'd only take the time to ask them. The challenge is getting all that competitive information out of the heads of the customer and the sales staff and into some kind of actionable form. The ways of doing that are many, but success comes when the program is intentional, well-managed, and most important, shared. The goal is to take data from diverse sources, and by piecing it together, paint a mosaic containing useful information.

The third best source is the competition. Sometimes just giving them a call and asking them what they are up to can do wonders in adding pieces to the competitive jigsaw puzzle. Quite often, in the process of maintaining competitive fitness, new business opportunities are discovered. By matching competitors' strengths with your company's weaknesses (or vice versa), you can form strategic alliances to better serve the customer and the future of your company.

Industry associations, meetings, conventions, and experts of both traditional and nontraditional competitors can also provide useful information that, coupled with the data gathered from the other sources, becomes very useful.

There are a number of competitive intelligence professionals who provide and maintain competitive intelligence programs for companies. Most of these individuals are highly ethical, creative-thinking investigators. But beware! Any inappropriate action by an authorized agent of your company could have devastating implications if it is discovered by others.

Most companies are not as intentional as they should be with their competitive intelligence gathering. Managers are often disappointed with the findings of customer research. They say that they already knew more than 80 percent of the information that was obtained. These doubters are not wise to the fact that it is from that 20 percent that was not known or validated that something useful will come.

Benchmarking

Benchmarking is a continuous process for measuring service, products, and practices against organizations recognized as leaders in the area of particular interest. Benchmarking looks at competitors and other companies with similar activities to find ways of elevating the quality of the work in your company. The benchmarking process consists of deciding what area of your business you desire to change or improve, identifying an organization with the desired performance level, observing and analyzing the way they conduct their process, understanding it, and then installing a customized version of the activity in your organization.

Though benchmarking may provide opportunities for improvement, keep in mind that adopting the good practices of others may put you even farther behind in the race. They've probably moved on to a better way! Benchmarking should never be used as a primary method for elevating performance, improving an activity, or redesigning a business system. Benchmarking must be viewed as one of several data points used by management for developing project missions and addressing other important challenges.

Core Competencies

The strategy to integrate the collective knowledge and the diverse skills with the multiple streams of information and technologies encompass the core competencies of the organization.

In the short view a company may derive its competitive advantages from the price and performance attributes of current products. In the long term, however, competitive advantages come from the ability to conceive the inconceivable. New-product and service advantages are realized from management's ability to recognize and consolidate skills and technologies into corporate core competencies unknown and unavailable to the competition. Most reasonably functioning businesses have the technical and intellectual resources for building core competency strategies, but top management often lacks the vision to recognize competencies or establish administrative processes for organizing the competencies and using them to the company's greatest benefit.

Core competencies is about unleashing corporate imagination and creating expeditionary missions into the future. Outcome management means envisioning markets that do not yet exist and having the ability to stake them out ahead of the competition. Identifying and creatively applying core competencies can be the single most important activity for building a future from the future.

There are three measures for identifying a company's core competencies:

- Does the competency provide potential access to a wide variety of markets? As an example, one of the core competencies of Sony is miniaturization. Bringing miniaturization to its products requires that its inventors, engineers, and marketing staff share an understanding of not only the technical possibilities but also the customer's needs.

- Does the competency make a significant contribution to the perceived customer benefits of the end product?

- Will the competency be difficult for competitors to imitate or benchmark?

Most companies that engage in the identification of core competencies discover no more than three or four. A list of a dozen or more invariably indicates that what has been identified are the key strengths and not the special market differentiators found in core competencies. Once the company has identified the core competencies, it must redesign its systems and processes to take full advantage of them. A part of that redesign is to build into the learning culture (training and education processes) a focus and emphasis on the core competencies.

ACTIVITY-BASED COSTING

Most companies are content in establishing success measures as comparisons against past efforts. The question usually answered by these measurements is, "How did we do?" Activity-based costing consists of processes and measures that answer, "How are we doing right now?"

Given the dynamics of commerce, continuing advances in technology, and the evolving desires of customers, traditional measures like process performance, customer satisfaction, and cost of quality are no longer sufficient.

Activity-based costing includes:

- Analyzing the value of activity or work—Focusing on the steps in a particular process, the resources each consumes, and how everything works or doesn't work together.

- Identifying cost drivers—Overhead is broken into batches of factors that cause work and determine the final cost of an operation.

- Analyzing competitors' similar processes (i.e., benchmarking)—Understanding your competitors' profitability as well as your own.

- Assessing sources of value-added activity—Deciding who does what in the most efficient and effective manner. One question that we often ask in the early stages of implementing the outcome management process is, "Can you differentiate between work done right the first time and rework?"

- Analyzing product/pricing relationships—Looking at product life cycles and value in relationship to current and future customer needs.

The one measure of the worth of an activity, system, function, meeting, or process is: Does the action add value for the customer and the company? This is a single measure that drives the outcome management philosophy. Identifying and eliminating non-value-added activity is often a very emotional process. Activity-based costing provides a narrow view of looking at costs and of associating costs with activities. Targeting activities as value-added or non-value-added becomes a separate issue with activity-based costing used as a data point in making the value decision. In an outcome management environment, deciding if an action adds value for the customer and the company is often best left to those involved in the process. Leadership's job is asking those in the process the questions, "How does this add value?" "If this were your business, would you be doing it?" and "Would the customers pay for it if they knew you were doing it?"

Activity-based costing is a way of looking at business operations in detail and at the results of an activity to create a more accurate, up-to-date picture of the economic benefits of the work that's going on. The methodology is particularly useful in valuing information technology because traditional accounting and costing measures often do not provide sufficient data on which to quantify the automation decision. By analyzing the value of small increments of the activity (i.e., the cost drivers), by looking at similar activities and their cost within a competitive operation (i.e., benchmarking), by costing steps as value-added and non-value-added, and then determining if the activity really is meaningful to the customer and the company, a manager can make a more reasoned decision. Too often decisions to automate are made based on the allure of high technology, when eliminating the process altogether would produce greater savings and improve performance. The detail of examining work through activity-based costing paints a picture in the present, whereas traditional costing, such as cost of quality, tells us only of past performance.

WHAT NEXT?

Though we have identified activity-based costing as one of the seven *strategies*, we believe it to be only a necessary step toward future-based costing. It is important to find ways of looking to the future for measures, and to use targets instead of experience or active measures for inspiration and planning.

SECTION III

Fire! Most Excellent Formula

"The good of a man is the active exercise of his soul's faculties. This exercise must occupy a complete lifetime. One swallow does not make a spring, nor does one fine day. Excellence is a habit, not an event."

—Aristotle

VOICE IN THE MIST

The fog consumed the night. Scores of tree frogs randomly punctuated the tense silence. Occasionally fragments of the fog would come loose and splash into the water and cause the young Iroquois' breath to quicken.

In the heavy darkness, he sat as still as the river in his birch bark canoe. His stomach ached with the pain of hunger. It had been six days since he had eaten. He survived only on water. Water was abundant.

The rains had begun 10 days ago, the very day he had entered the forest, and had stopped a few hours ago at sundown. The rains had drenched his spirit and totally washed away the thrill of the excursion. He was in the dark, in the mist, and in despair. This was his initiation into the hierarchy of the tribe—the survival test—and all

161

hope of success had been washed away by the torrential rains.

On the fourth day, while building a shelter with his small canoe and limbs from fallen trees, he found a nest of rabbits and caught two of them. Their pelts hung from his loincloth. It was impossible to build a fire, so he ate them raw. Only a portion of the unpleasant meal had stayed with him. The experience was almost as bad as not having eaten at all.

There were 10 more days to go. He had begun the 200-mile journey of initiation with his knife, his bow, six arrows, the birch bark canoe, and a small knapsack that contained a line and a hook for fishing, a small pouch of ceremonial smoking weed, and a pipe. Yesterday as he sat helplessly in the deluge, he realized that the small bag of belongings had been lost. Though the items were not necessities for survival, the loss of them represented his plight and drove him to the edge of his confidence. The next day he discovered that three of his arrows were flawed and useless. That discovery furthered his hopelessness.

The ceasing of the rains brought out the snakes, poisonous lizards, and spiders. So he found safety in the isolation of the canoe resting on the dark waters of the swollen stream. Fear of the reptiles and insects in the night was not his nature. It was a sign of his despair.

The sounds from the frogs and the fog dripping into the stream established a rhythm in his mind that lulled him into a shallow sleep. He saw his mother holding a child; his brother as a boy, chasing a boy; and he saw the face of a chief. The face was unfamiliar, but somehow known to him. The face was carved and crevassed with lines of wisdom. He and the chief did not speak, but they communicated. The young man asked the deepest of all questions and the chief replied with the wisest of all answers.

The rhythm, silence, and sleep were broken by the crash of limbs. The young man, though startled by the sound, began to breathe more deeply than he had in days. His eyes searched the darkness. Nothing could be seen.

He reached into the bottom of the rain-filled canoe and found his bow. It felt familiar in his hands. His spirit began to rise. He looked for an arrow. Nocking the arrow into the bow he waited. The frogs had stopped. The fog was quiet. His heart was the only sound he could hear. Suddenly the night crackled again with breaking limbs. He shot the arrow into the night. He never heard it land. His stomach gnarled. His heart stopped. The despair began to creep back into his mind.

A familiar but unknown voice called to him from out of the forest, from out of the night. "Aim higher and slightly to the left." The voice frightened him, but he quickly retrieved another arrow from the dampness of the boat. He raised the bow and followed the instructions. He held steady and fired. Silence. The voice said, "Center your courage, your wisdom, and your soul."

The young man was suddenly no longer afraid. He thanked the unseen moon for the challenging experiences of the past few days and became energized with the life or death situation in which he found himself. His past, present, and future hung in the balance, on the accuracy of the flight of a single arrow.

He placed the arrow on the rawhide string, raised the bow high above his head, and with fluid, confident action lowered the bow until his hand touched his cheek and his eye was sighted down the unseen arrow. He fired into the darkness and heard a simultaneous thud and moan, the signal of his arrival into the leadership circle of his people.

He moved the canoe toward the quiet by pulling on the branches that hung above the stream. When the canoe hit the shore, he reach forward and felt the familiar antlers of the fallen deer. He dragged the deer into the boat. Using it for a pillow, he drifted off into a deep and confident sleep. The morning would be soon enough for feasting. The night would bring rest and quiet celebration.

CHAPTER 12

The Ultimate Strategy— $E = mc^2$

"No problem is solved from the same consciousness that created it."

—Albert Einstein

ENERGY AND MASS

A body has a greater mass while moving than it does while sitting still. The force of a train moving at 100 miles an hour is greater than the force of the same train at 35 miles an hour. A company that is rapidly moving toward its vision generates more energy than a company that is moving only at the current speed of commerce. The fast-moving company can convert this additional energy into additional speed to reach the vision quicker or into time to expand the vision. A company that is moving only at the current speed of commerce is headed to oblivion.

Several years ago a CEO went to his bank to borrow $5 million for additional operating capital. We accompanied him on his presentation to the bank's lending board. Our job was to explain the new quality-based management philosophy we were helping him deploy and to reference the market study in which we had participated. His company is a home health-care provider.

One of the bank board members asked about the company's growth rate over the past three years. The CEO told the bankers it had been in excess of 20 percent. We validated the number. The bankers were impressed. A question they didn't ask, however, was, "How fast is the home health-care industry growing?" To which the honest reply would have been, "Thirty-two percent per year." Another even more important question the bankers didn't ask was, "What kind of growth rate will the industry experience in the next three years?" The relationship between the growth of the company seeking the loan and average industry growth should have been a major factor in the banker's consideration of the loan.

If a company within a growth industry isn't exceeding the industry average, that company isn't doing something right. In this particular case, the CEO was able to use the management philosophy change and the cash infusion to eventually exceed the home health-care industry's growth average. The bankers, however, made the loan based partially on the answer to the wrong question and were lucky that their decision turned out to be a successful one. The bankers didn't understand the relationship between mass and energy.

RELATIVITY

To the scientist, energy and mass are the two constants. Energy is defined as the released force of power. Energy can be harnessed—hydroelectric power—or it may go unharnessed—the Los Angeles earthquake of 1994. Energy in nature is released as motion, electricity, sound, or heat.

Mass is defined as material substance or matter. Mass in motion is energy. There are three physical states of mass: solid, liquid, and gas.

Einstein expressed this mass (matter)-energy equivalence through his famous equation $\mathbf{E = mc^2}$. $\mathbf{E}$ is the energy equivalent to $\mathbf{m}$(mass), and $\mathbf{c}$ (electromagnetic constant) represents the speed of light. Einstein called mass frozen energy or rest-energy. When mass moves, energy is created. Water falling with great force from the side of a mountain creates motion. When turbines are placed into the rush of the falling water, more energy is created by their spin. Connect the spinning turbines to transformers and the rushing water becomes electric power.

The bankers didn't look for the right energies on which to base their loan decision. By making the loan based on unrelated comparables, like general economic conditions or, "The last guy in here asking for money was doing only twelve percent growth; this guy is doing much better," the bankers were taking a great unknown risk. By not concerning themselves with the future of the home health-care industry, their risk was significantly increased. In fact, many financial business decisions are based on rest-energy— what's already in the bank—rather than on what the future holds—the potential of the energy when released.

EXCELLENCE

The quality management movement in this country didn't begin with a focus on quality; it began with a focus on continuous improvement. Once the concept of continuous improvement finally took hold, quality became the byword. Today, the word is excellence—beyond quality.

Precepts

The guiding precepts presented in chapter 2 were discussed in a negative framework; Excellence, however, comes from turning the negatives of those precepts into positive forces of energy from management. Hold to and commit to the principles expressed in them, and excellence will become a habit instead of an occasional event. Imagine a workplace where excellence is so ingrained in the philosophy and actions of everyone that errors and mistakes become the events to be celebrated. Imagine a culture where failure is viewed as a fortuitous learning experience. In such a culture, there will be greater opportunities for success, for everyone will feel free to take informed chances. The precepts in a positive framework are as follows:

- Visionary leadership drawn from the future and executed through clear and challenging missions.

- Guidelines for actions that allow for failure as well as innovation.

- Focus on the business of the company in an environment that demands continuing organizational adaptation to the changes in that business.

- Openness to ideas, cooperation, and a loyalty to the system as a whole.

- Rewards based on the desired behavior, most often on collaboration.

- Allegiance to the future as the primary source of knowledge and measure.

- Recognition of education as a part of work.

- Commitment to continuing improvement and organizational change.

- Integration of vision, mission, work, and measure.

- Valuing input over output when measuring results.

Excellence begins at the top. Leaders and managers who learn and live these precepts set the attitude required for excellence to permeate the entire organization.

MASTERY

Mastering the important tasks of leadership, decision making, and visioning is key to successful outcome management. Mastery is not a familiar word in today's business vocabulary. Mastery sounds like something that will take too long to do. Sadly, much of what was practiced in the name of quality management did not demand mastery of leadership, decision making, and visioning and therefore did not prove very useful.

Several of the allegories presented in this book are about master-student relationships. Outcome management demands that the leader of the company and eventually everyone else in it become masters of their fates. It's the only way to ensure a future. The reason we devote considerable space to the discussion of education and training is that most leaders' biggest complaint is that they can't find the time to get smarter at what they do. So they continue to rely on experience and on their intuition as the drivers for future success.

Success, however, comes from mastering the collection, creation, and application of new wisdom. Collection and creation are the byproducts of unconventional thinking—going to new and different sources for stimulation and inspiration. Application is knowing when it feels right, then doing it—intuition. Intuition, however, is not a static attribute. It can be improved and it becomes a very powerful instrument when sharpened through self-education, coaching, listening, and dreaming.

Modes of Consciousness

There are two modes of consciousness: intuitive and rational. Most busy executives turn to the rational for answers. Rational answers are based on experience and recall, and therefore come easier and more quickly than intuitive answers.

Have you ever noticed, when you begin to explain a new idea or theory to people, their mind starts searching for a familiar mental box in which to place it? When they first repeat what they've just heard (as opposed to what you just said), they attempt to reduce your communication to the familiar.

For example, talk to someone about outcome management and he or she will say, "Oh, that's sort of like TQM. We tried that, but it didn't work. We did get some good ideas out of it though." Yes, outcome management is built on the quality discipline. But because the listener reduces your communication to its perceived essence and reaches a conclusion about your message, that message becomes more difficult to get across.

The type of listening cited here is linear and rational listening. For the most part, the listener turned off the intuitive side of his or her mind—without even knowing it. Even as the communicator, we assume that a space exists just behind the eyes of the person we are communicating with, where our message is received and stored. We talk into that space instead of observing the reactions of the listener and adjusting the message to meet the listener's understanding of it. (We imagine a similar space inside our own heads from where we are talking.)

Trusting Intuition

Placing information in mental boxes before processing it through reason *and* intuition devalues the lessons to be learned and the knowledge to be gained. In our consulting engagements and our writings, we've learned to better trust our own intuition, as individuals and as collaborators. Quite often one of us will ask the other for a specific output, only to receive something entirely different. The mental processing usually begins with the rational side,

"What in the world is this? This is not what I asked for!" Whereas some collaborators might get angry, upset, or figure that they must have miscommunicated, we open ourselves to the intuitive side of listening.

We say to ourselves, "He wouldn't have said this if he didn't think it was worthy of my attention." We don't always agree, but the quality of our work is constantly elevated from using both sides of our individual and collective minds.

As with the yin and yang of leadership and management, rationality and intuition must be balanced. Masterful leaders know when to lead and what to manage. They know how to balance empowerment with control, seriousness with humor, and recognition with corrective action. Each of these actions can produce a positive or negative result when properly or improperly applied. Not one is negative in and of itself.

What is bad and harmful, though, is giving preferential use of the rational action over the intuitive action or vice versa. We do not, in any fashion, mean to minimize the importance of being rational when it is appropriate. The following provides examples of the yin and yang of effective thought and action.

Yin	Yang
• Intuitive.	• Rational.
• Responsive.	• Aggressive.
• Cooperative.	• Competitive.
• Contractive.	• Expansive.
• Impulsive.	• Analytical.

The rational side always looks for answers inside time and experience. The intuitive side looks outside time and into the cosmos. Experience, for example, is one of many rooms in the rational side of the mind where knowledge is collected and stored. In the intuitive side, experience resides in one large room with all the other potential sources of knowledge.

Think back on your own greatest insights. Didn't you arrive at them in some mysterious or haphazard fashion? Einstein said that many of his best ideas came to him so suddenly while he was shaving that he had to move the blade of the straight razor very carefully each morning, lest he cut himself with surprise. Learn to master the intuitive side of your mind in much the same fashion as you have already mastered reasoning.

Mastering Tools

In chapter 10, we presented the theory behind the natural learning process. Learning is a process acquired through the use of one or more of the five senses, sight, sound, touch, taste, and smell, and in each learner one of these senses is dominant.

We've found that the best and quickest way for a leader, manager, or anyone else to become proficient in a skill, technique, or tool is by experiencing and sensing with their dominant learning mechanism, which requires a customized learning process. This concept often flies in the face of company training directors. They are accustomed to going to the shelf to find something they can teach, rather than developing customized processes from which the student can learn. This customized learning usually requires bringing in a master.

The following are the basic steps of the NLP approach. NLP provides lasting and rewarding results for leaders or managers who want to learn a skill, methodology, or technique. Imagine you are trying to learn a new activity (e.g., a sport or craft) as you read the steps:

1. Choose a skill and an expert (master).

2. Gain wisdom from the expert.

3. Model the pertinent physiology (map the way the expert does it).

4. Determine your dominant senses and your perceived limits.

5. Model the expert's mental strategy (what goes through his or her mind).

6. Form a model of the expert's actions and feelings.

7. Mold your actions to fit the model.

8. Experience the skill under as close to actual conditions as possible.

9. Review, practice, and refine your model of the actions and feelings.

10. When it feels right, do it!

Observation Is the Key

The most important aspect to the use of the natural learning process is observation. As you or any student views experts in the performance of the activity, try to determine if the experts actually do what they say they do. Often the activity has become so subconscious the experts are unaware of the dimensions and dynamics inherent in their actions. The experts may be driven by patterns of which they are unaware. You are looking for the true critical path.

You are looking for the differences that make a difference. When charting or modeling the expert's actions for the first time, make sure you use the expert's words to describe the actions—not your own. This proves useful when discussing the activity with the expert. It is also important to form a hypothesis about what is going on in the expert's head during the performance of the task and to discuss that with the expert as well.

Through a detailed study of the thought processes and physical movements of the master, a student can find the critical path to success. Modeling the patterns of the master increases the opportunity to become truly proficient in the activity.

The natural learning process is very effective when learning complex subjects like activity-based costing, cycle-time compression, and other mathematical-based methodologies. NLP is also effective when learning a visioning process, elevating planning skills, and developing processes for changing organizational culture.

CULTURE

Getting and maintaining the right attitude, adopting a system view, becoming vision and mission driven, rewarding collaboration, and focusing on the business instead of the organization are other keys to successful outcome management.

Quality management, for example, is basically an advanced manifestation of the prevailing management theory and practice, but even it is linear in its approach, narrowly focused as far as results are concerned, and analytical—with a tendency to measure categories and deal with only one important issue at a time.

Outcome management, however, is nonlinear—moving out to the future for information, answers, and challenges. It focuses on the entire business ecosystem as a whole, instead of just on one or two parts at a time. Outcome management recognizes that no problem can be solved from the same consciousness that created it. To achieve excellence requires the creation of a new consciousness from which to think and a new culture in which to work. The primary goal of any organization should be its own self-destruction, that is, to have the capacity to recreate itself. The organization's culture must celebrate change and constant renewal.

Getting the culture and the attitude right are fundamental to success. Quality management systems sometimes failed because the process of implementation was viewed as additional layers of activity and not recognized or rewarded as a part of work. Culture *kills* processes that threaten its continuity.

$E = MC^2$

We have borrowed Einstein's theory to connect the important forces of business success. Our version is: excellence = mastery $\times$ culture^2. A company in which everyone is committed to excellence, dedicated to mastery, and operating in a dynamic culture is a company moving toward its vision with speed, purpose, and enthusiasm.

The E represents excellence as the fundamental mode of existence in today's and tomorrow's dynamic marketplace. Excellence is beyond quality. Quality has become a given.

The m is the symbol for mastery of the expanding methodologies found in the outcome management philosophy and other knowledge sources.

The c stands for the culture in which work is created, performed, and measured. An effective work culture is one that celebrates and rewards collaboration, contribution, learning, and results.

Excellence and mastery are equivalents and constants that when incorporated into a dynamic and vital work culture create motion, light, and heat. $E = mc^2$ is the success formula.

Just as the water cascading down the mountainside can be harnessed to produce power and energy, so can the forces of excellence and mastery be combined to produce the illumination and momentum required to see the future and make it what you desire it to be.

CHAPTER 13

Predicting the Future—
Outcome Management

"Our folks don't expect something for nothing . . . they want to win so badly they just go out there and do it!"

—Sam Walton

SELF-MOTIVATING ATTITUDE

Winning is defined by the desired outcome. Winning as a team is possible only through collaboration. Collaboration occurs when everyone is rallied around a single vision and is to receive a fair share of the spoils of victory.

Visionaries create winning combinations of undertakings, collaborators, and prizes. The late Sam Walton could read the passions of his customers, knew the hearts of his employees, and was willing to share the spoils of his victories.

Sociologist George Steiner said, "If an organization is managed by intuitive geniuses there is no need for formal strategic planning. But how many organizations are so blessed? And if they are, how many times are their 'intuitives' correct?" In the case of Walton, it was most of the time. He appeared at every store opening until his failing health prevented it. Sam Walton was not there primarily to see the customers either. He was there to be with the employees. He'd have everyone get to the store very early and would lead them in a march through the store. He'd shake every hand and tell each employee just how much he or she meant to him.

Walton personally selected the store sites. One of his criteria was putting them close to where his potential employees lived. Walton chose a niche in the market where the only difference between the customer and the employee was the red vest the employee wore while on duty. The demographics of the customer and the employee were the same. He created customers by creating jobs for them. Through his intuitive genius, Walton was able to establish a self-motivating community of followers who'd follow him anywhere. By sharing the fruits of the labor, he created more money for himself than anyone could imagine and more millionaires than any other enterprise ever had. Walton followed the first rule of effective leadership in the outcome management environment: If it feels right, do it!

Emotion and participation in the glory create a self-motivating attitude within an organization, not rhetoric, promises, vacillations, or fear. The first question that you as a leader must ask is, "Do you want to win?" If the answer is "Yes," then you have to decide what winning means to you.

WHAT IT TAKES

Winning requires a systemwide self-motivating attitude. The right attitude is created from confident leadership, a collaborative environment, an empowered workforce, and loyalty to the customer and the company. The attitude becomes self-motivating and self-perpetuating when the leadership is trusted.

Dr. Deming said, "The aim of leadership should be to improve performance, increase output, and simultaneously bring pride of workmanship to employees. The goal of leadership is not to find failure, but to remove the cause of it—by helping people to do a better job with less effort."

The great leaders of history shared some basic characteristics. They were bold. They believed in the rightness of their causes. These leaders were restless, were dissatisfied with the status quo, and aggressively sought change for the better. Despite many setbacks and disappointments, they never seemed to waiver in their quests. These bold leaders were willing to change everything but their values and their goals. But most of all, they were trusted by their followers. Their followers believed in the vision and became committed to the cause through trust in the leader. Trust is the emotional glue that binds followers and leaders together. That binding through trust is what drives collaborators to a self-motivating attitude.

Enthusiasm feeds off enthusiasm. Ideas bounce off other ideas. Tension, release, acceleration—unbridled energy is then harnessed and focused on attaining the common dream.

SELF-BUILDING FOUNDATION

Attitude alone won't get it. Your team can be fired up and highly motivated but you can't win the basketball game unless there is a goal and a ball. Section II included discussion of the seven strategies we selected as being fundamental to the leader's toolbox—technology planning, time reduction, quality discipline, knowledge culture, competitive fitness, activity-based costing, and system redesign. When addressing challenges and developing new opportunities, the leader must apply these tools or strategies to the issues at hand. They must be considered as a whole and not as separate activities. These strategies should be thought of as guidelines or outlines for behavior—not as parameters or arbitrary constants. Through integrated yet flexible application, the strategies become self-building blocks, always in a state of advancing development. When, as in most companies, these strategies are applied singularly, the effect is unpredictable and the potential for dramatic improvement or change is diminished.

For example, take the prevailing theme of business in the 1990s: doing more with less. Let's assume that your company has chosen that theme as an "I want." Obviously one way to do more with less is through automation. Looking at automation would be a part of the technology planning process. But what you automate is driven by the current and future demands of the customer and on the company. Those drivers are incumbent to competitive fitness and the system redesign commitment.

The goal of automation is to accelerate the activity in the value-added steps and to eliminate non-value-added steps altogether. Saving time is the purpose of the time reduction strategy. The initial cost of automation and its eventual payoff fall under activity-based costing. And what are the new knowledge requirements that will come from automation? Those strategies are a part of the knowledge culture activities.

The strategies are interactive bodies—electromagnetic forces that attract, repulse, pull, and react to one another like the forces in all living systems. It is through constant interaction that they become self-building and remain dynamic and vital to the success of the business.

SELF-FORMING STRUCTURE

How do we know we are headed in the right direction, topside up, and at the desired speed? How do we know our fuel is burning efficiently and giving us maximum torque? The key coordinates and gauges of business are those elements that we identify as structure components—futures, missions, values, success factors, measures, and synergistic actions. These components are the framework or references for knowing where you are and how you are doing, and for making the adjustments to get back or to stay on course.

In a traditional business environment, the structure components are used to calculate speed and direction. In an outcome management system, the structure components are self-adjusting, self-forming sensors that calculate and adjust simultaneously—like the Japanese washing machine that uses fuzzy thinking to sense the characteristics of the wash load and change the agitation and displacement of the water to provide the optimum results.

The future will not stand still for the planning process to be completed. The plan may even become obsolete before it is completed. Whatever the plan, the activities of the plan will have to be adjusted to meet the demands of the changing future.

Create a mission, appoint a mission team, and develop a mission plan. Chances are that during the development of the mission plan the mission will change.

Establish value based on the image and personality of the organization and on what's important to the organization.

Identify the success factors by which the attainment of the vision will be quantified. And if the organization is moving enthusiastically toward the dream, those original success factors may seem naive.

Build a set of mission measures and watch them grow and change as the mission moves forward.

Through the encouragement of synergistic actions, people begin to collaborate because collaboration produces the best results and synergistic actions become rote and subconscious.

IT'S THE SYSTEM!

F.A. von Hayek said, "Many of the greatest things man has achieved are not the result of conscious, directed thought,

but the result of the combination of knowledge more extensive than a single mind can master."

The concept of a company with a self-motivating attitude, self-building strategies, and a self-forming structure
is built on a system view—that is, looking on the whole as
being greater than the sum of its parts. Outcome management is looking for the new, not rehashing the past. It is
also looking at everything as one, and remembering that
everything causes everything else.

Growth in a company comes from understanding the
interrelatedness of activities, strategy, and attitude—system
thinking, planning, and acting. System thinking means
anticipating the diverse effects of contemplated actions. System planning means building a future on outcomes, instead
of from current processes and biases. System acting means
integrating all work through a single measure: How does
this activity add value for the customer and to the company?

The key to successful outcome management is deciding
on the desired future and then addressing everything at
once in order to achieve that future (see Figure 20). In an
earlier chapter, we pointed out that one difference between
outcome management and traditional management systems is that outcome management focuses on system
thinking, instead of system analysis.

Outcome management begins by building ideal systems
from the future. An ideal system is defined as: *procedures that
are organized, integrated, and conducted in a manner that produces the best result for the customer and the company.* System
thinking requires that you be creative with your thoughts,
always consider the big picture, and eventually go with
your gut. Hold to the philosophy: I'll do it if it feels right.

NEW WORLD BRAVE

Whenever people are permitted to fail, excellence occurs.
Managers and employees who are not allowed mistakes

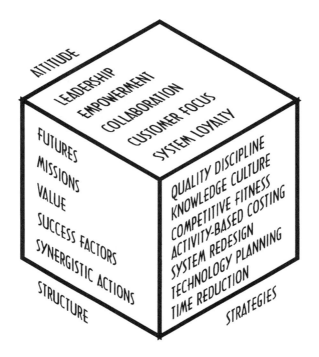

Figure 20. The System

will not take risks. Exceptional futures are the product of risk taking. Smart leaders provide the vision, the tools, and the culture in which their followers can carry out missions without fear of failure. Bravery is a desired attribute in a business setting.

Trace Die Cast, Inc. is a small manufacturer of auto transmission covers and electric fan castings, located in Bowling Green, Kentucky. Its owner is Lowell Guthrie, a retired engineer from the Ford Motor Company. When Guthrie retired, he decided to build a die-casting plant. Instead of buying an existing company, he wanted to build one from the start. Guthrie was a long-time student of Deming's philosophy of business and wanted to start pure, with no history.

He first traveled the United States looking for the perfect site. He selected Bowling Green, Kentucky, because of its favorable business tax benefits, convenient location, its proximity to several automobile assembly plants, and because the trade school in Bowling Green had an exemplary record for turning out quality-conscious workers.

Guthrie purchased a site and then hired his manufacturing team before even building the plant! During construction he engaged them in extensive training, and when the building was complete, he used his manufacturing team, under the leadership of experienced professionals, to install all the equipment.

Once the plant was opened and operating, Guthrie posted the monthly financial statement on the breakroom bulletin board for all the world to see. Trace Die Cast has been in business successfully for more than five years.

On a recent tour of the plant, we were astonished at the cleanliness and order. The place was bright, cheerful, and very businesslike. We noted the control charts posted at each work station. On passing a young woman assembling casting for an electric fan, we noticed a line with a very high peak on the chart. "What happened here?" we asked. The young woman replied, "Oh that was the day I shut down the entire production line including the furnaces. While working, I noticed what appeared to be cracks on three castings within a period of twenty minutes. I sensed something was wrong and pulled the whistle to stop production. The plant engineer found that the thermostat on the furnaces was not operating properly and the temperature was below the requirements for a quality cast. We were down for the rest of the day."

Lowell Guthrie not only encourages his people to go with their intuitions, but he demands that they do so. Like the Iroquois brave who fired his final arrow at the unseen target, this young woman risked her reputation on her intuition—on what she felt to be the right thing to do. Agreed, it was her leader who empowered her with the knowledge, information, tools, and culture that minimized the risk she took. At Trace Die Cast there is no fear of failure, just an expectation of excellence.

INFLUENCING THE UNINFLUENCEABLE

The five factors that impact business success include the two uninfluenceable factors—the customer and the business ecosystem and the three influenceable factors—attitude, strategy, and structure. Most business leaders do fairly well addressing the influenceable. In the old seller's market days, people and companies got rich addressing the influenceable factors, without a clue as to what the future might bring. In today's dynamic marketplace, developing the vision and mission and structuring the work before you understand where you're going and why will only lead to disaster. How in the world can you develop a business plan, marketing plan, or long-range plan without beginning the process with predictions of the business ecosystem and where the customer will be in the future?

In reality, it makes no difference where the company wants to be. What makes the difference is being where the customers are going to be, with what they want, when they want it, at a price they're willing to pay. Implied in the outcome management philosophy is that any vision or set of "I wants" is drawn from a rational and an intuitive examination of what the future may hold.

If the future were just a deck of cards, visioning would be the ability to predict the probability of the various hands that could be dealt. That's the rational side of the visioning process—examining the probabilities. The other side of visioning has to do with intuition—examining the impossibilities. Thinking of things no one else is thinking of. In our case it was outcome management. Other business advisors are on similar tracks. Much of what we've presented here is presented in bits and pieces elsewhere.

There's an old saying that goes, "Never read a book written by someone who has written more books than he has read." We've read the books. We worked hard to understand the prevailing philosophies and reviewed the good and bad practices of others (and ourselves). But, through it all, we've found that the real wisdom in our thinking and writing, though stimulated by others, has come from that unidentifiable inner source, and at unpredictable and sometimes inopportune times.

The processes of unconventional thinking, multidimensional thinking, system thinking, dreaming before we think, and other ways of thinking presented here are processes we use as a part of our daily routines as writers and as coaches. Creative ideas are the fruits born from the tangled vine of conscious and unconscious behaviors, rational and intuitive thinking, and from continuity and discontinuity.

Though the ideas and methodologies collected here are new, different, or presented with our unique spin, many of the basic concepts of outcome management can be found in a book written by Peter Drucker, *The Age of Discontinuity,* published by Harper & Row in 1969! In that epic tome, Drucker predicts our present.

Drucker was predicting in 1969 what our business ecosystem would be like now and what we'd need to do to meet its challenge. Read Drucker's book. It will provide you with illumination of what must be done to achieve business success in these turbulent times and validate much of the material presented in this treatise.

THE TWO FUTURES

Outcome management as a business philosophy establishes two types of future for any company in business today: to be or not to be. To be means developing an early warning system for the change that will take place. Not to be means continuing to focus primarily on the present.

If you lead a company or have worked for a company for a long time, ask yourself these questions: Has this company's original vision come to pass? If it has and a new vision hasn't taken its place, how will success in the future be possible?

Too many leaders and managers spend too much time in the present. There is no future in the past, and there's very little future to be found in the present. Granted, the present must be attended to, if there is to be a future. But without any time allotted to dreams and thoughts of the future, the present will soon disappear. Successful leaders and managers are those who know just how much time they need to devote to the present and how much to spend with the future.

CHAPTER 14

Reference Point—
Transforming the Future

"What is essential is invisible to the eye."

—From *The Little Prince* by Antoine de Saint-Exupéry

WHAT'S KI GOT TO DO WITH IT?

Ki is defined in a Japanese dictionary as mind, spirit, and heart. Though the Japanese dictionary lists hundreds of expressions that use the word ki, the most widely known use of it is in the martial arts and in Oriental medicine. In these contexts ki refers to a subtle form of vital energy. Ki is the life force; a source of internal strength. Ki is a universal energy that can be directed, but it is not something that can be measured with an instrument.

Every shred of scientific evidence points to the unity of body and mind, but in our western culture we most often act as if they are separate. Ki is that mysterious quality that allows us to determine if we feel healthy or sick. Physical objects present no barrier to ki, yet it has the power to move them.

A company's success is dependent on its ki—its spirit and its actions—on its mind and body working in concert. You might say on its vital energy. Through its ki, a company is able to tap its vital energy resources when everyone is focused or centered on its vision.

An appropriate balance of spirit and action is required to achieve phenomenal business success. For a company to reach that proper balance there must be communication—not just oral communication, but clear, concise written communication. The strategic plan is where the company's spirit and actions become one. If the plan is challenging, lively, dynamic, pointed, directed, and accountable, the company's ki will grow in strength and move the entire company to ever higher performance. If the preparation of the plan is only an excuse for the executives to go to a nice resort for golf on the expense account, ki will weaken and the potential for achieving the vision will dim and disappear.

Though some leaders are more comfortable working mostly on the action side of business endeavors, more and more successful business people are giving credence to the need to balance action with spirit. In his 1994 annual report letter, G.E. Chairman John F. Welch reviewed G.E.'s progress through its three operating principles, which he identified as boundaryless, speed, and stretch.

"G.E.," he says, "is using those principles to build a workforce with an absolute capacity to improve everything. Stretch at G.E. means using dreams to set business targets—with no real idea of how to get there. If you know how to get there, it's not a stretch!" G.E., in applying its version of outcome management, has learned that incremental improvement goals neither inspire nor challenge anyone. G.E.'s stretch philosophy is manifested in its mission to introduce more new products over the next two years than it developed over the past 10 years.

"Concentrating on speed," he says, "means that new products are coming out with drumbeat rapidity. There is a new-product announcement from our appliance division every ninety days!" Welch says the concentration on speed has freed up nearly five million square feet of manufacturing space in the past three years.

The boundaryless notion at G.E. means erasing the lines between management, operations, R & D, and marketing. It means gathering collaborators and co-conspirators from across disciplines into one room, with one shared coffeepot, one shared vision, and one consuming passion— to design the world's best jet engine, ultrasound machine, refrigerator, or whatever the customer needs.

He says there are two ways to lose your job at G.E.: commit an integrity violation or be a controlling, oppressive manager who doesn't draw out the energy and creativity of those managed.

Strategic planning has taken on a new meaning at G.E.. Welch and his team have adopted the wisdom of the ages that says success comes when you: Dream before you think, think before you plan, and plan before you act.

"THE PLAN, BOSS, THE PLAN!"

A successful strategic plan focuses on the future, sets a clear vision, presents challenging missions, and demands total commitment to energetic collaboration from those who plan the work and those who perform the work. The plan must set forth the necessary actions and establish the right spirit.

A traditional plan is structured as follows:

- Statement of purpose.
- Industry analysis.
- Market analysis.
- Business background.
- Organizational plan.
- Operational plan.
- Marketing plan.
- Competitive advantage.
- Financial.

OUTCOME MANAGEMENT
BUSINESS PLAN

A business plan in an outcome management environment is organized around vision, missions, key system objectives, and outcomes. It is dynamic and living, not an inert reference document. The outcome management version of a business plan includes:

- Vision point—Developing and creating the desired future.

- Data point—Collecting, reporting, and analyzing the information and knowledge required to drive the planning.

- Decision point—Developing and planning the missions to achieve the vision.

- Action point—The actual work required to advance the plan.

- Turning point—Evaluating progress and direction to adjust the vision or the actions for achieving it.

- Transformation point—The experience of success that elevates achievement beyond the original vision.

Each of these is discussed in the following sections.

Vision Point

In the words of G.E.'s John Welch, visioning is "using dreams to set targets." Outcome management challenges the leaders to dream before they think, think before they plan, and plan before they act. In a successful outcome management environment, the leader must know more about the future customer and the future business ecosystem than about any other issues pertinent to the life of the company.

Creating a meaningful vision for the company paints a picture of what the customer will look like in the future with the marketplace of the future as the background of the picture. That picture is the target. It is best painted through a series of "I wants," not in an esoteric statement. The vision point is where the leader sets the destination for the company.

Setting a vision requires looking to the future for challenges, deciding what will be required to address those challenges, then assessing what resources you have in order to determine what additional resources you will need.

Data Point

The data point is where information, knowledge, and resources are collected, reported, and analyzed as to the value each might add to the forthcoming journey. Traditional management systems look first at the resources in order to determine what kind of opportunities or future can be made from them. In outcome management the vision is set before examining the resources.

The subpoints of useful data to be examined are the vision measure data, customer tracking data, system and key system performance data, work culture data, work process data, state-of-technology data, and internal and external competitive fitness data. The review and examination of these different dimensions of the data point provide the knowledge and information needed to identify the value-added resources on hand and the resources that must be acquired to achieve the vision. There is no mention here of marketing, operational, administration, or financial data per se. That information is gathered, but in a horizontal or integrated fashion as related to each of the previous subpoints. These subpoints are different but similar expressions of the strategies, the structure components, and attitude characteristics discussed throughout the book. Once the data point assessment is complete, it's time to move on to the decision point.

Decision Point

Deciding what missions are required to advance toward the vision is the responsibility of the senior planning group. Armed with a clear vision of future performance requirements and sufficient knowledge of current performance and resources, the senior team creates missions. The decision point is where the written portion of the plan is developed. In a traditional management environment, the decision point is called strategic planning.

Action Point

The missions developed by the senior staff require various types and levels of collaboration. A complete redesign of a key system, for example, would require a project team made up of persons from across the entire spectrum of functions within the organization. Another mission might be no more than a probe into possible new products or services, which might be assigned to an individual. Since a goal of outcome management is to turn routine work over to machines or eliminate it altogether, most work in organizations of the future will be brainwork. As a company progresses to higher levels of achievement, projects and missions will constitute most of what will be defined as work. In the early stages of deploying outcome management, however, project participation becomes one of several aspects of work, and to be successful a company must recognize and reward the execution of project work in the same manner as routine work.

Turning Point

Another role of the senior planning group is to monitor the actions of the organization to ensure that performance, progress, and possibilities are maximized. Since the plan and the work are organized around missions and systems, and not by department, the senior team measures results in collaboration, not as internal competitors or as department heads. If the work or the use of resources is not being maximized in the quest toward the vision, adjustments are made. If a mission has identified a new challenge or uncovered an important upstream issue that needs to be addressed, the scope or direction of the mission may be changed. If the work has brought the vision into question, the vision is revisited and, if necessary, it is changed.

Transformation Point

As an organization moves toward its vision through missions and key system redesign projects, changes will be necessary in the way work is performed and in the way the organization is structured. An underlying principle of outcome management is that form follows function.

The company is viewed as a system with two parts—its business and the organization. Organization is the form. Business is the function. The organization is the structure in which work takes place. The business is the outcome of work. Success comes from restructuring the organization to meet the needs of the business. Trying to find the business to meet the needs of the organization is no longer effective. That style of operation died when the market shifted from supply to demand.

Transformation of the structure is the final step in effecting successful change, achieving excellence, and reaching the vision. Once transformation takes place, anything is possible.

"In a company that now rewards progress toward stretch goals," says Welch, "rather than punishing shortfalls, the setting of these goals, and quantum leaps toward them are daily events. Such targets are making seemingly impossible goals exciting and bringing out the best from our teams." The environment described by Welch is the kind of environment we describe as having been transformed. It is an environment driven by the corporate ki; the company's universal energy is directed, centered, and focused like a surgical laser on the future. A transformed company, like the Iroquois brave, fearlessly fires its arrows into the darkness of the future and listens for its own voice to correct the aim. "Aim higher and a little to the left."

BUSINESS PLAN EXAMPLES

Vision and Decision Point Examples

Following is an introductory letter written by the CEO of a company that uses a home-grown version of the outcome management business planning process. The letter is followed by the CEO's "I want" vision and the missions developed by the senior staff to advance toward the vision.

> Dear Colleague:
> For the past 11 months the senior staff of our firm has been working with great energy and dispatch to elevate our abilities to lead BOLIVAR into a fruitful future for us all.
> We began this process last January when James Edwards joined our staff as vice-president of marketing. Shortly thereafter, we secured the service of an outside management consulting team to assist us with our education and planning. When we began the development of a new management system for our company, we first looked at total quality management. After consideration of several types of quality management processes, however, we determined that the best course of action was to develop our own system, rather than to adopt someone else's process.
> During the first two months, I developed a set of statements that, when considered as a whole, paint a picture of

what BOLIVAR will look like five years from now. I call them my "I wants." Collectively my "I wants" form a vision statement. Not the typical pie-in-the-sky vision statement like in the past, but a very succinct set of aspirations from which all work will be measured and on which all planning will be based.

Following the development of my "I want" vision, the senior team and I engaged in a week-long mission-development planning session to create missions that will lead us to achieving the vision.

The processes of developing the vision and the preparation of the missions were not secretive or exclusive. Most of you have already played a role as information gatherers and knowledge sources. Though I have already thanked you personally for your efforts, I thank you again as a team.

This is the very first truly active and living business plan that I've ever been privileged to participate in developing. This plan represents a real beginning of the new way we will conduct business from now on. If you do not share this belief with me, you soon will. That is a guarantee.

Our industry is in its infancy. Today we are in the materials separation and recovery business. Tomorrow we will be a primary source of raw materials for industry. Today we are focused on our technology. Tomorrow we will market wisdom and our technology will merely support our efforts.

To ensure that everyone has a clear understanding of what "I want" for us, I have included my aspirations for the future in the introduction of this business plan. The senior staff will also meet with you to clarify your understanding of my vision.

This is an exciting time in our growing industry, but more particularly in our company. I look to the future with you, as we honor accomplishments. But there is no future in the past. Continuing success will come to us only as we think and plan from the future. And as we do so in a spirit of enthusiasm, collaboration, and trust.

Thank you,

Fred Hubble

Fred's "I Wants"	Explanation	Measure	Missions
1. I want everything we do to add value both for the customer and to the company.	Adding value is why each of us is here. Our sole responsibility is to add value to the work and to pass it along to our customers—internal and external. If an action, an idea, a process, or a decision does not add value for the customer and to the company it is unworthy of consideration.	Value is measured against the requirements of the customer and the vision and missions set forth by me and our senior staff.	**Mission A:** To regularly collect and distribute, throughout the organization, all relevant information regarding the customer's current and future wants and demands. **Mission B:** To establish and continually communicate a clear vision from which to measure the success of all missions, goals, and objectives.

Fred's "I Wants"	Explanation	Measure	Missions
2. I want a system that rewards collaboration. The Lone Ranger doesn't work at BOLIVAR.	We must have a system that rewards collaboration, instead of one that promotes internal competition. We are in this together. What is good for all. The reward for accomplishment is a successful company. Special contributions by individuals will be recognized, but only those who collaborate will be significantly rewarded.	Performance reviews will be based on contributions to the system's performance, on collaborating with and supporting coworkers, and on the value one adds to the work. The organization's support of the employee will be a part of the evaluation process.	**Mission C:** After one year's study and planning, the company's reward and recognition system will be changed to reflect the emphasis on collaboration. **Mission D:** The company's senior team will personally conduct training in and understanding of collaboration, especially teamwork.

Fred's "I Wants"	Explanation	Measure
3. I want a system that fosters creativity and initiative, encourages constructive dissent, and is open to change and opportunity.	We will eliminate fear of failure. Everyone will be encouraged to take risks and try new things to add value for the customer and to the company. Improvement comes from experimentation, not from whimsical directives. Ideas must be tested, however, before we carve them in stone.	The attitudes of managers and the atmosphere of the workplace are the true measures of a fear-free system. The willingness to debate, defend, and be persuaded with hard data is the mark of a spirited and open organization.

Fred's "I Wants"	Explanation	Measure	Missions
4. I want BOLIVAR to be known as the innovator in the automated waste recovery industry because of our ever-expanding knowledge.	Ours is an industry in the making. To achieve this goal, we must adopt a strategy that focuses on the needs of the marketplace and not on our technical expertise and our proprietary technology. We will continue to learn how to better apply our expanding knowledge to customer needs. We will be accountable for the continuing and successful operation of every product we sell.	The measures of our success will be customer satisfaction, a collaborative and spirited workplace, and profitability.	**Mission E:** We will accelerate exposure in the marketplace to our good deeds, satisfied customers, and our vision for the industry. **Mission F:** We will improve our communication with one another.

Fred's "I Wants"	Explanation	Measure	Missions
5. I want BOLIVAR to become obscenely profitable within the next five years; and for every share-holder, manager, and employee to participate in the profits.	The opportunity is before us. To achieve this lofty goal, we must work in collaboration, tear down depart-mental barriers; and tap all the brain-power available to us.	Profits, growth, and continuity.	**Mission G:** We will develop a learning culture that ensures that every-one has the knowledge, infor-mation, tools, and culture with which to achieve his or her potential as an individual, employee, and member of the BOLIVAR team. **Mission H:** We will create an accounting tracking system that provides current, rather than historical, information for decision making.

Data Point Example

The following is excerpted from the business plan of an international company that operates with a version of an outcome management business philosophy. Vision measurement data, customer tracking data, system and key system performance data, work culture data, work process data, state-of-technology data, and internal and external competitive fitness data were collected and analyzed by the senior staff and others. The information presented is from the summary and conclusions of the data-collection process. Though the summary and conclusions were developed from analyzing the full body of information collected, the primary sources on which each assumption is based are listed in parentheses:

SUMMARY AND CONCLUSIONS
1. A system view of an organization looks horizontally across directorates, functions, and departments, beyond internally generated boundaries, focusing on sets of interrelated activities that have a defined output for an identified customer or customers (customer/system performance/work process).
2. Our discussion with a number of exceptional companies indicates that the adoption of a system view, when planning and implementing improvements and changes, will increase the opportunity for significant business gains (vision measures/system performance/competitive fitness).
3. We will, therefore, operate within three key systems—order fulfillment, product introduction, and support services (customer/system performance/work process).
4. Each of these key systems will comprise processes and functions that will form the links of the delivery chain that connect work with outcome. The majority of employees will work within these processes and functions, where their work will be directed to the support of the key system mission. Each key system will have a designated system owner who will sit as a member of the executive staff (customer/system performance/work culture).

5. A small number of people will work in processes that serve and support the whole business, providing infrastructure, setting professional standards, and monitoring policies that apply across all areas of the business (work process/work culture).

6. The adoption of this system view is fundamental to achieving our vision. We will plan around our key systems, operate within them, and measure our achievements from the output of each of them and of the company as a whole (vision measures/system performance/state-of-technology).

7. Where restructuring is proved to be necessary, it will be done only after analysis and proper planning. Changes will not be made in the organization's structure until business outcomes have been established (system performance/work culture/state-of-technology).

8. We estimate that we will achieve full deployment and operation of this key system strategy in the third quarter of 1996 (vision measures).

Decision Point Example

The future is made by the decisions you make today. The senior staff of a company takes the vision of the leader and develops missions to achieve the vision. This process is generally referred to as strategic planning. The decision point is where the missions are committed to paper, mission leaders are determined, teams are organized, and special project ownerships are assigned. The following are missions developed by various kinds of companies:

- Cycle-Time Mission—To reduce the order-to-delivery time of power transformer metering devices from 10 to 3 weeks.

- Key System Redesign—To serve our retail customers with the knowledge and strategies needed for them to convert from tobacco shops to gift shops. Changing our company from a distributor of products to a marketer of inventory management and marketing expertise.

- System Redesign—We will structure all work within key systems, thereby eliminating department functions. There are considerable qualitative benefits from operating within key systems, including improved capability to act, compete, survive, and prosper. Operating in key systems, rather than through departmental functions, will accelerate new-product development and introduction and provide flexibility to reorganize and restructure. Focusing on key systems will require absolute role clarity and the elimination of all the non-value-added activities that do not support our vision and missions. Working through key systems will require that everyone see his or her job as doing whatever is necessary to enable the key system team to achieve its goals. The resulting benefit will be that the customer will be assured of a rising standard of products and services.

Action Point and Turning Point Example

In the early stages of deploying an outcome management philosophy, much of the new work is collaborative and teamwork. These new activities are added to existing activities. Another aspect of deployment, however, is the reduction and eventual elimination of rework, redundant work, and other non-value-added activities, thereby freeing people for meaningful involvement in the new collaborative activities. Here is the first quarterly status report on the results of the actions being taken by a company's executive committee to advance and secure their one-year objectives.

1993–94 OBJECTIVES
DECEMBER STATUS REPORT
Action: To use the outcome management philosophy to
understand and establish customer needs. We will measure
the improvement of all items associated with meeting the
needs of the customer.

- Fred Jones, group vice-president of commercial operations, has presented a list of needs and wants from our
  primary customer, our company's sales and marketing
  division. This list is being prioritized for our use.
- In October, 30 members of our manager group met
  with the major distributor of our products to learn
  more about their requirements. (Note: In this company
  the marketing department is identified as the primary
  customer and distributors are considered to be the customers of the marketing department.)
- An internal customer awareness day has been sched-
  uled in March of 1994 for our plant in Alabama.

Action: We will develop and post scorecards of business
indicators that can be seen by all our associates by October
1993.

- Scorecards are updated monthly and posted in five
  commons areas throughout the plant on the following
  measures: backorders, OSHA recordables, spending,
  batch record errors, reworks, exception reports, and
  miscellaneous customer comments.

Action: We will complete a skills and knowledge needs
assessment for all associates by November 1993.

- Our company has conducted the needs assessment and
  will make its final curriculum redesign report at the
  February meeting.

Action: We will initiate our new training and education
program by March 1994.

- This objective is on target.

Action: We will continue to stress the importance and visi-
bility of our safety program while developing new performance goals for the organization and specific functional
areas by November 1993.

- An annual goal of no more than 24 OSHA recordable injuries has been established for the entire manufacturing operations. To date, 13 have been recorded.
- In December, engineering received the first CEO's award for outstanding achievement in health, safety, and environmental management.

Action: We will develop and implement a communication and involvement program to ensure that each associate understands and participates in the outcome management deployment initiative.

- An associates involvement mission was developed in September, and a team was empowered to develop the communication and involvement plan. The mission team has submitted draft objectives and actions to be reviewed by the executive committee at its January meeting.

Action: We will maintain a flat or reduced cost of manufacturing for each of the next five years.

- Our expenses through December are at 94.6 percent of budget and consistent with our five-year projections.

Transformation Point Example

In the successful redesign of a key system and the successful transition to a system view of the company, the last things that happen are the application of technology and the restructuring of the organization to meet the requirements of the new way of operating. Many companies make the mistake of applying technology and downsizing or restructuring the work before establishing the vision. Outcome management is a mirrored version of the traditional manner in which many leaders approach the processes of business.

Figure 21 shows how the outcome management philosophy differs from traditional management activities. Traditional management often begins with assessing and changing the organization and ends up building a vision on basically historical data. Outcome management begins,

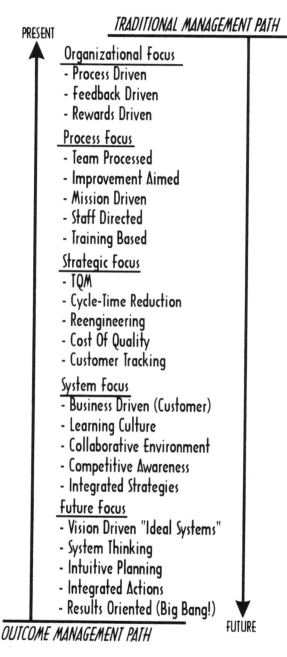

Figure 21. Traditional Versus Outcome Management

in the words of G.E.'s John Welch, ". . . with a dream" and ends with restructuring the work to meet the vision. Form follows function.

Transformation requires more than the traditional TQM-type path of continuous improvement. Here is a statement developed by one of our clients that expresses the value of including a change track along with the improvement track found in quality management disciplines:

IMPLEMENTATION PROGRAMS
The company's planning framework explains at a broad level how the areas for change have been identified and selected and how change programs will be monitored and reviewed. Implicit, however, in the making of any improvement in our business performance is our escalating ability to successfully manage and implement major change initiatives.
Our existing change (or improvement) programs are now implemented on functional and departmental levels and carried out under the heading of waste elimination. These activities must continue, as they form the basis of our continuous improvement culture. Where step changes in performance are required, however, this bottom-up, evolutionary approach will not serve our business interest.
Although change challenges will each be very different in nature from improvements, success will also require the use of a consistent approach and common methodology. One such approach has been successfully used in a number of areas within our organization—business performance improvement (BPI). We have decided to continue with the BPI as our agent of change and for implementing the major change programs that are a part of this business plan.

OUTCOME MANAGEMENT
SUMMARIZED

Here is some outcome management wisdom from the book. Read carefully as you look both at the present culture of your company and to the future as you might desire it to be.

- There is no future in the past.

- Five basic factors affect business success—customer wants, the business ecosystem, the company's business strategies, its values, and its attitude.

- Strategies, values, and attitudes are easily influenced. Customer wants and the business ecosystem are not.

- The leader must know as much about the customer as does anyone else in the organization.

- The leader must set the course for the future from the ability to predict what the customer will want and what the business ecosystem will demand.

- Outcome management is the act of causing—inductive reasoning—not the act of reaching a logical conclusion—deductive reasoning.

- A company is a system with two parts: Its organization is the structure in which work takes place. Its business is the outcome of work. Success comes from focusing on business instead of on the organization.

- The primary goal of any organization must be change.

- System thinking replaces system analysis in outcome management.

- System thinking means anticipating the diverse effects of contemplated action.

- Every activity must add value for the customer and to the company simultaneously.

- The role of the leader is to vision or model ideal systems from the future.

- Dream before you think, think before you plan, and plan before you act.

- If it feels right, do it.

- A leader's vision is best expressed through a set of clearly articulated "I wants"—not through some esoteric vision statement.

- Missions are the projects that support and advance the vision.

- Outcome management demands a balance of leadership and management.

- Outcome management works in a collaborative environment. Collaboration is more than teamwork.

- You always get the type of behavior you reward.

- People are best led to higher performance.

- Successful companies operate with a family view of the organization, share wisdom throughout the company, demand collaborative thinking, and integrate all work.

- Empowerment is leadership's providing the knowledge, information, tools, and culture with which everyone can perform and improve work—in accordance with the company's vision and missions.

- Outcome management is based on the leader's creating a vision, establishing universal trust, and gaining full commitment from everyone in the company.

- Outcome management requires a dual-track approach for addressing opportunities and challenges. Incremental improvements are addressed on the organization track and big bang key system redesigns are the responsibility of the business track.

- Go for the big bang.

- There is no quality steering committee in outcome management. That role is the responsibility of the senior staff.

- The most effective way to teach is to find out how the student learns.

- A key system is that collection of work that goes into a significant business-producing activity.

- Key systems are made up of functions and processes.

- Outcome management implementation begins with awareness and understanding, moves to empowerment and deployment, and continues through realignment and transformation.

- Consultants and coaches should be heard and not seen.

- Outcome management planning begins with "What do we want?"—not "What can we make out of what we have?"

- The theme of doing business in the 1990s is doing more with less.

- Successful outcome management requires multidimensional system thinking and a balance of rational and intuitive thinking.

- Pushing anywhere on the system causes reactions throughout the entire system.

- Attitude includes confident leadership, a collaborative environment, an empowered workforce, customer focus, and system loyalty.

- Strategies include quality discipline, knowledge culture, competitive fitness, activity-based costing, key system redesign, technology planning, and time reduction.

- Structure components are futures, missions, values, success factors, measures, and synergistic action.

- Outcome management requires an equal emphasis on training and education. Training is for meeting the demands of today's work. Education is for meeting tomorrow's work demands.

- In an ideal system procedures are organized, integrated, and conducted in a manner that produces the maximum results for the customer and the company.

- A company that is rapidly moving toward its vision will generate more energy than will a company that is moving only at the current speed of commerce.

- Learn to use your third eye.

- Listen to the voice in the mist.

- Always look for the differences that make a difference.

- Take your time before you begin change; be impatient thereafter.

- No problem can be solved from the same consciousness that created it.

- Stay balanced in all that you do.

- Excellence should be a habit, not an event.

CHAPTER 15

Being Is More Powerful
Than Becoming

"It ain't braggin', if you can do it!"

—Dizzy Dean

FORGET YOURSELF . . . NOT

Suzuki Shosan, the Zen master, was a samurai warrior who gave up arms, around 1600, when peace finally came to strife-torn feudal Japan. Many of his contemporaries of this period also became Zen masters, and like Shosan laid down their arms and turned to education and healing. Some former samurai, however, remained perpetual competitors while others like Shosan moved on to these more contemplative and venerable pursuits.

The ancient Zen masters of both camps agreed that self-centered virtue was often a far worse condition than self-centered vice. "Piety is often clothed in acceptable appearances," they said. Their belief was that the unreflective individual is not under pressure to examine personal behaviors. Under these conditions it is much easier to become set in one's ways, fortified by a self-perpetuating circle of rationalizations and justifications. Though some of his contemporaries took a more balanced approach to piety, Shosan expressed his more pointed view this way:

"There is virtue in not stagnating. People get fixated at one point or another, with the result that they are unaware of what went before or what comes after. Thus they lack virtue. In their

livelihood as well as in their perceptions of others, they lose much for little gain. They are, however, unaware of this in themselves. So if you want to leave the small for the great, notice your fixations and detach from them." The great wisdom contemplated by Shosan and his fellow travelers down the path of Zen often provides simple, yet profound truths that are applicable to modern times. The responsibility of running a company or leading people in pursuits of goals can be a heady one. Those of us charged with such responsibilities must regularly examine our motives and behaviors, if we are to be true to our calling. We must not fall prey to our positions or become set in our ways at the expense of the goal, to the discomfort of our associates, or to the detriment of our own self worth. By fixating on the present we can lose respect for the humbleness of our beginnings and the exhilaration we will enjoy in the collective achievement of the goal. We can expend the energies of our associates and ourselves with very little to show for it.

Shosan provides this simple, profound truth to leaders: "So if you want to leave the small for the great, notice your fixations and detach from them." He concludes his wisdom for leaders with this counterpointed admonishment:

"Forget yourself, yet don't forget yourself. When people are ambitious and greedy, they are concerned exclusively with themselves, forgetting even their own relatives."

"On the other hand, when in pursuit of what they like, they forget themselves and lose their conscience, so they do not understand the implications of what they do and are unconcerned about even the direst of consequences. Much unworthy behavior derives from this, so don't forget yourself."

CONCLUSION: HOW YOU START

It was about 7:00 P.M. Just as we arrived at the conference center meeting room, the media technician was unlocking the door. The room was ready for the opening event of the week-long planning session. At one end of the room was a video monitor, a flip chart and a large sign *"Ready? Aim.*

Fire!" At each of the 25 places at the table were the usual accoutrements—pad, pencils, and water glass. There were two additional items at each place not usually found at planning events: a throw-away 35mm camera for each participant to record events as they unfolded; a Playskool crossbow with three Nerf arrows.

"I thought this was some kind of executive gathering," said the technician.

"It is," we replied.

"But what are the crossbows for?"

"You'll see."

Besides ourselves, only 2 of the 25 participants had any idea of what was about to happen—the company quality director and its CEO. The purpose of the event was to kick off the company's new management initiative based on the principles of outcome management. The senior management team gathered for the event was made up of highly skilled and educated, independent individuals, including the CEO. The average age of the group was 36, quite young for persons of their positions and responsibilities. This was definitely a "Ready? Shoot! Aim." crowd. And everyone was accustomed to shooting at the targets of their choice, usually at each other. But all of that was about to change.

EPILOGUE

Dreams of the Future

"I am captivated more by the dreams of the future than by the history of the past."

—Thomas Jefferson

COTTONWOOD JESSE

Jesse took one of the wooden barrels off the running board of the old truck and doused a corner of the fire. The blaze hissed and faded. "Don't know why I wasted good water like that," he murmured, "could have used my boot."

He sat back down, took one more drink of the cold coffee, and crawled into his bedroll. "I'm damn lucky this stuff was in the back of the truck," he said out loud. There was no one else to talk to. Most times Jesse liked having no one to talk to, but this was not one of them.

Jesse is a cowboy. But in these times, being a cowboy isn't as much fun as it used to be. Back East, Hoover's Depression really seems to be taking its toll. Out here in Skellytown, Texas, things in general aren't so bad, that is unless you're a cowboy. But Jesse is a cowboy. It's the only thing he's ever been.

He was on his way across the flats to his brother's house near McLean when his truck broke down. Jesse doesn't like trucks, but these days even a cowboy needs a truck just to find work. His brother had left a message for Jesse at the general store in Skellytown. It seems his brother's boy had hurt himself on the combine and they needed to go to Amarillo in the morning to see if anything was broken.

The brothers didn't talk directly, but Jesse's brother wouldn't be concerned about him not being there until it was time to go. And since Jesse wasn't known for his punctuality anyway, they still wouldn't be concerned.

Jesse knew he could fix the truck at daylight, so he wasn't worried about that. But he was worried about something—the future. He wanted to get to his brother's before supper so he could talk to him about what the future might hold for a fading old cowboy. That's why he wasn't looking forward to being alone. Thinking about the future made him scared. Cowboys don't like being scared.

Besides his bedroll, Jesse had brought along some jerky, flour, and fatback. The jerky and flour were for just such an emergency and the fatback was a gift for his brother. He made some tortillas and a white jerky gravy with the provisions. That was a meal he was usually fond of, but tonight it made him a bit sentimental and sad. The concoction was basic trail food, but there wasn't much of a need for trail food anymore. There isn't much of a trail left, with the truck lines and the railroads taking over.

Jesse had camped just off the dusty road cut, in case someone might come by. But he knew better. The flats were a shortcut, but they were also dangerous. Most folks took the gravel road that went over to Pampas and down to McLean. It was about 10 miles farther that way than the 30 miles straight across the flats from Skellytown.

The flats are for the most part a leathery-looking mud that can look dry. Dig down about two inches, however, and the ashy surface becomes damp and greasy. Come a rain and a deer could get mired down to its knees and die there. What roads there are in the flat are service roads for the few telegraph, telephone, and electric wires strewn across west Texas.

The night sky was velvet. There are more stars on a clear night in Texas than anyplace else on earth, and from his vantage point in the bedroll Jesse could see them all. Jesse could also see the darkened rambling shapes of cottonwood trees off in the distance. But what he couldn't see was the future.

He could also see the single strand of a telephone wire, running high alongside the road cut. The wire knew just where it had been, and just where it was going. Jesse knew where he had been, but had not a clue as to where he was going. Jesse looked at the wire with envy.

"Figuring out the future," thought Jesse, looking at the stars, "is just about as easy as pulling an armadillo out of a hole by its tail."

Jesse turned on his side and went to sleep in the cowboy way—one eye closed and the other partially open to guard against the uncertainties of the night.

He awoke with the first streak of dawn.

"Why is it that boiled campfire coffee tastes so much better than home brewed?" Jesse wondered as he raised the hood of the truck.

Mornings belong to cowboys, ranchers, vermin, and farmers. Even at the beginning of a bad dog-hot day, there's a cool time. A signal that the day can be what you make it, that you don't have to become consumed by the heat or beat down by the work. Embracing that philosophy has sustained many a cowboy and others who labor long in the hot Texas sun.

The eastern sky was streaked now with oranges, grays, and yellows. A light wind ebbed and fanned the fire. A roadrunner traversed the camp on his way to a rattlesnake breakfast and a coyote howled a final goodbye to the fading moon. Jesse examined the engine of the five-year-old Dodge truck—rusty from conditions more than from time. And he tried to think about the future.

"Probably just a dirty magneto switch or the plugs," he said to himself, tapping the alternator. *"Guess I need to take it down." About 15 minutes later, Jesse found a scorpion inside the alternator—fried and mangled. He took out each sparkplug, scraped the gunk off with his pocket knife, tossed his gear into the truck bed, covered the water barrels on the running board with canvas, and climbed into the cab. Jesse turned the key, but the spark was low.*

Jesse hates trucks. He is a cowboy. "Never had trouble like this from a horse. Hell, you can even talk to a horse," he thought. *"No way you can talk to a truck."*

"One more shot," said Jesse, putting the truck in neutral. He stepped out onto the ground and, with one hand on the steering wheel and the other on the door frame, began to push the truck along the road cut. After about a 25 foot running heave from Jesse, the old engine started on compression, jerking and snorting Jesse and the old truck toward McLean. There were about 20 more miles to go.

On the 45 minute ride Jesse tried to turn his thoughts to the future. All he could see was the present, a present swarming with machines. Machines are changing the world. Jesse doesn't like machines. He doesn't know anyone who does. But they are taking over work. Trucks and trains are putting an end to his livelihood, combines are replacing families in farming, and automobiles are making horses antiques. People are flying around in machines.

"Where is this world going to," he questioned himself, "and what's going to become of me? I'm almost forty-five years old. Don't know how to do anything but cowboy."

He could see the smoke rising and smell the biscuits when he was more than a mile away from his brother's farmhouse. Jesse and John aren't close. They help one another out from time to time, but mostly just because they are family. Cowboys, for the most part, think that becoming a farmer is just one step from becoming city-fide. So, Jesse and John never talk on the subject of farming.

"Hey, Uncle Jesse, have a good trip?"

"Usual. How's your arm, boy?"

"Still hurts a bit," said the young boy, holding out his arm trussed in a homemade sling.

"We still going to Amarillo?"

"Daddy says so."

"Come on in, Jesse," said John. "Sarah's cooked up some fresh beef in your honor."

"Hey, Jesse," hollered Sarah, "I'll be in there in a minute." Sarah came into the room with a cup of home-brewed coffee in a porcelain cup. "It's good to see you," she said, handing him the cup. She gave him a hug. It was always a surprise when she did that. He never knew just what to say or do. "Breakfast will be ready just as soon as the biscuits come out of the oven."

Jesse couldn't talk about what was bothering him in front of the woman. They talked about the trip to Amarillo—how long it would take, when they expected to return, and what they'd do while they were there. Jesse said mostly, "Yes." "No." "Don't know." He did thank her for the breakfast and then quietly refilled the water barrels on the running boards from the well in the side yard.

Standing out by the truck, Jesse asked the boy to go back into the house and get four bandannas. The boy obliged. They climbed into the cab of the truck with the boy in the middle. Jesse said, "Now you all take one bandanna and tie it around your neck. Put the other one in your pocket. It gets too hot to ride with the windows down, but if you don't cover your mouth and nose, the dust and the sand will choke you. You'll know when to put it over your face"

"What's the other one for, Uncle Jesse?" asked the boy.

"The heat. You'll need it just as soon to wipe the sweat off you."

The truck started fine. The boy waved at his momma and off they went to Amarillo. The ride to Amarillo was about 70 miles, with Groom a little less than half way.

The boy had been to Amarillo a couple of times in the wagon, but never in the truck. In fact, he had only ridden in a truck once before, when they'd gone to see Jesse in the rodeo at Pampas. It was new then and Jesse took them all for a short ride.

The Texas sun was hot, the dust was thick, especially until you got to Groom, and conversation was difficult with the windows down. They rode in silence. If someone saw something that might be of interest, he'd point. The others would look, usually without acknowledgement.

The road from McLean to Groom was gravel and dirt. From Groom to Conway, however, you ran into asphalt and gravel; from there for the next 15 miles into Amarillo, it turned to concrete.

About 15 miles out, just past the Alanreed settlement, there is an unusual natural phenomenon that passersby usually stop to see—Cannibal Springs. Jesse slowed the truck to about 10 miles an hour and the dust began to disappear. "Want to stop at Cannibal Springs?" he asked.

"Never passed it by," said John. The boy obviously liked the idea as well, but he didn't speak.

As the dust cleared, a trail of vapors became visible on the horizon. "There it is!" exclaimed the boy, "Yonder." A jackrabbit zigged across the road.

It was Jesse who had told John about Cannibal Springs. He had first seen it on a cattle drive to Abilene.

He stopped the truck about 50 feet from the springs, parking it under a stand of scraggly cottonwood trees that line a bone-dry creek. They walked down to the springs and into the mist created by the bubbling waters. The stream is about two feet wide and runs swiftly with hot white rapids randomly scattered about. You can hear the boiling and rage of the water. Alongside are lucid green pools lined with mineral deposits.

"The spring is caused by a crack in the earth. When rainwater or an underground spring hits them hot rocks, it brings up minerals. You look at a miner's map and a hot

springs map and they'd look pretty much alike," John lessoned the boy.

"You mean there might be gold here?" asked the boy excitedly.

"Might be," said, Jesse, "but probably not enough to fool with. Fall in one of them pools, though, and you're cowboy stew," smiled Jesse. It was his first smile in weeks. "That's why they're called Cannibal Springs."

The boy had heard the story before, but he enjoyed hearing it from someone other than his dad. "You ever seen anyone fall in, Uncle Jesse?" asked the boy, knowing the answer.

"Never saw no one fall in directly, but I met a man one time who had fallen in. It warn't no pretty sight."

"What did he look like?"

"Face looked just like a horned toad," said Jesse. "That's what he'd come to be named—Toad."

"Can I walk down there where the stream disappears?"

"Go 'head, son, but we need to get back on the road." Jesse and John turned and headed for the truck.

"John, I don't know what I'm going to do," Jesse blurted out.

John was taken back with the fear he heard in the statement. "What do you mean, Jesse?"

"Cowboyin'. There ain't no work."

"Times is changing, Jesse, and they're changing fast. It seems like the things that always got you through just don't work no more. There just ain't no future in lookin' back. Sometimes it seems like hard work and experience don't count like it used to. Everything is new."

"It's them damn machines. Everywhere you look, they're replacing people."

"Yeah, I'm saving up for a tractor. The way prices is, I can't make a livin' on the 20 acres I farm now; need to be farming 30! These days you've got to be able to do more with less. More crops, less help."

Jesse dipped the tin cup into the water barrel and handed it to John. "When you're gettin' slower and the world's getting faster, it's hard to figure out what to do next. I don't know nothin' but cowboyin'." John didn't know what to say.

"Here, boy, have a drink. We've got to get on the road." John was glad the boy came up when he did.

Back in the truck, they rode in silence, each with one bandanna tied around his face and the other in his hand to wipe away the sweat.

As they rode, Jesse reflected in the comfort of the past. He could smell only the sage and the greasewood that dotted the barren landscape along the dusty road. John was held in the anxieties of the present by the odoriferous emissions of the aging eight-cylinder combustion engine under the hood of the rusty truck.

The boy had closed his eyes in a daydream—hypnotized by the hum of machinery, captivated by the wonders of nature, and energized by the uncertainty of what the future just might hold.

FIVE SUCCESS FACTORS

In the world of commerce there are five factors to a successful future—understanding what people want in the way of goods and services, understanding the forces of economics and politics, working in ways that are efficient, working in ways that are effective, and having the right attitude toward work and the people who will benefit from your labor. Success comes only to those who rightly predict the changes that will occur in the demand for goods and services and in economics and politics. And who then are wise enough to adjust their work effectiveness, their efficiency, and their attitudes to meets the changes as they occur.

If you lead people in any endeavor, it is your responsibility to lead them toward the future. As trite as that sounds, many in leadership positions haven't a clue as to what the future will hold. They operate only in the present with knowledge, information, tools, and cultures created in the past. There is no future in the past. Not anymore.

Technology has changed the world forever. Technology has changed change. Change has become virtual instead of linear, requiring new ways of predicting it and new ways of addressing it. Outcome management is a call to all who lead people in business, government, academia, and families to learn to look to the future for answers, instead of to the past. There is no future in the past. Not anymore.

COTTONWOOD TREES

The cottonwood tree grows mostly along rivers and streams. Its thick, dull gray bark splits into ridges and long furrows. Its whitish or light brown wood is soft and well suited for making furniture, crates, and barrels. The cottonwood will grow tall, if the stream is free and ever-flowing.

In west Texas, however, most cottonwoods are thick, knurled, and short-lived. Twisted by the wind, worn down by the dust and dirt, and forever thirsty, even though they consume water like running fountains. A cottonwood can never get enough water. In fact, environmentalists, farmers, and cowboys will tell you that if you want the stream to serve the continuing needs of the land and the people, the cottonwoods have to go.

The best way to address the future is often to eliminate those things that stand in its way.

Decide first on the future you want for yourself and your company. Then, remove all the barriers that stand in your way. That's the essence of outcome management.

APPENDIX

Getting Started—A Guide
to Launching
Outcome Management

THE VISION:
THERE IS NO FUTURE IN THE PAST

The successful implementation of outcome management depends on a clear and challenging vision of the future. The primary task of a leader or a manager is to provide that vision, based on informed predictions of what the future will hold. There is no future in the past. Business success can no longer be found in attempts to replicate old accomplishments. The dynamics and the pace of change are too rapid and chaotic to depend on the present even as a driver for change. Success is possible only when the missions of the company are driven by the future needs of the customer and the future conditions of the business ecosystem.

If the leader's vision of the future is not clear to those charged with achieving it, work becomes drudgery, fruitless, and a waste of everyone's time. The visioning process is part science, part art. It is not just daydreaming, though that is an important aspect of it. Visioning is educated guesswork. A powerful vision is the key to successful strategic planning.

The most useful way for a leader to express his or her vision is through a series of clear, simple statements called "I wants," not through some well-crafted esoteric statement. Those platitudinal paragraphs written by the public relations department have never communicated the wishes of the leader to anyone. It is easier to understand a list of 20 thoughtful "I wants" than a vague four-sentence paragraph.

Begin planning with a vision. Never begin the planning process with an assessment. An assessment is merely an examination of past and current practices and accomplishments. The past and present are not appropriate drivers for planning. If planning is begun with an assessment of current activities and resources, the tendency is to attempt to build a successful future from that which is currently available. If planning begins, however, with an understanding of the future of business and the future needs of customers, there are no parameters as to what is possible. Once the predictions are made and the "I wants" set, then look at current practices and resources, and establish a value for each to achieve the desired future.

Questions for You

- Do you know what the future has in store?
- How did you or will you find out?
- Do you know what kind of future you want for the company?
- How did you or will you decide?
- Does your company have a vision or mission statement?
- If so, what does it say to you?
- Do your employees know what you want from them?
- How do you know?

- Are the things you want for the company both challenging and possible?
- How do you know?

Questions for Others

- Do you know what your leader or manager expects from you?
- If so, how do you know?
- Does this company have a vision or mission statement?
- If so, what does it say to you?
- Has the future for the company been expressed to you by leadership?
- If so, do you buy in to what you've been told?

THE MISSION:
FORM FOLLOWS FUNCTION

Once the company's leadership has painted a picture of the desired future and has gained the commitment of the other leaders in the organization, it's time to turn the vision into specific missions. This is the process that is commonly called strategic planning. Strategic planning, or any planning for that matter, is no more than developing the most appropriate path for the future and creating the right attitude within the organization toward the work to be done.

Planning in the 1990s must be business (function) focused, not organization (form) focused. Outcome management means first deciding what business you're in, then adjusting the organization's structure, strategies, attitude, and resources to address the demands of the business.

Missions are futuristic accomplishments drawn from the "I wants" vision of the leadership. Every mission has a different scope, unique parameters, its own significance, and must add a specific increase in value for the customer and the company. Missions may be carried out by individuals or teams. Make sure the assignment of a mission is appropriate for the type and amount of energy that is required to complete it. Don't ever create teams to do the work of an individual.

The purpose of a major mission, like the redesign of a significant business system, is to create a new system that will exceed the expectation of the customer and dramatically increase the value of the company to its owners, leaders, and associates.

Questions Regarding Missions

- Does this mission address one or more of the "I want" vision statements?

- Do we understand how the success of this mission will be determined?

- Is the mission clear and achievable?

- How will the customer and the company be served by the completion of this mission?

- Are there sufficient and appropriate evaluators to ensure the success of the mission?

- Do we have the knowledge, information, tools, and culture needed to successfully complete the mission?

EMPOWERMENT: THE KNOWLEDGE, INFORMATION, TOOLS, AND CULTURE

Effective outcome management requires that every employee be given responsibility for making the entire organization work better, not just for seeing that his or her job is done. When teams are formed to address missions or projects, team members must come to the task with a system view and without concern for departmental issues or fear for the need of self-preservation. Organizations must be flexible and continuously focused on meeting the needs of the customer and the company, not on protecting the current pecking order and maintaining the status quo.

Empowerment begins with communicating the vision, establishing trust, and gaining commitment. It moves forward through missions, projects, and assignments drawn from the vision. Empowerment is leadership's providing the knowledge, information, tools, and culture required to perform and improve work—in accordance with the company's vision and missions.

Knowledge is that body of intelligence inside and outside the organization needed to make wise and creative decisions. Information is defined as routinely useful data that everyone needs to stay on track, on task, and on vision. Tools are the techniques, processes, strategies, and technologies required to perform at peak efficiency. Culture is the context in which work takes place.

Questions for Everyone

The following questionnaire is directed to the employees of the company. Though each statement begins with "Our company is very good at . . . ," the process is in reality an assessment of the company's leaders and managers. Share this assessment with your employees without fanfare and collect the results anonymously. Complete the assessment yourself (along with others in leadership positions), but fill it out as you expect the employees to complete it. Besides providing you with a picture of how your employees see you as an empowerer, the gaps between what they say and what you thought they'd say will tell you something about how well you perceive and communicate. Study the gaps.

QUESTIONNAIRE
Indicate your opinion of each statement in the following
manner:
1 Strongly Agree   3 Somewhat Agree   5 Disagree
     2 Agree   4 Somewhat Disagree   6 Strongly Disagree

Our company is very good at . . .
☐ 1. Acquiring and using technology.
☐ 2. Introducing new technology to the workplace.
☐ 3. Adapting to new ideas.
☐ 4. Encouraging innovation throughout the organiza-
       tion.
☐ 5. Listening to new ideas from all organizational levels.
☐ 6. Communicating within the organization.
☐ 7. Providing training and education for everyone.
☐ 8. Using the future in planning.
☐ 9. Gathering customer information and using it.
☐ 10. Knowing what it takes to keep customers happy.
☐ 11. Creating unique products and competitive advan-
       tages.
☐ 12. Gathering and using competitive intelligence.
☐ 13. Providing clear project mission statements.
☐ 14. Committing resource to projects.
☐ 15. Creating time for dreaming, thinking, and planning.
☐ 16. Reducing and eliminating rework and redundances.
☐ 17. Responding to the needs of employees.
☐ 18. Encouraging collaboration.

WORK AND REWARDS: PEOPLE ARE
BEST LED TO HIGHER PERFORMANCE

The overriding purpose of outcome management is to
erase the lines between management, marketing, and operations to create a holistic focus on the system. Those lines
were unnecessarily placed there to serve the organizational
interest, not the interest of the customer. When the entire
company is viewed as an integrated, living system, barriers

begin to fall, unnecessary work disappears, and the magnitude of each achievement increases.

Outcome management, unlike traditional TQM, focuses the methodologies for addressing improvements and changes on results, not on the processes for achieving results. It is usually a waste of time to break work into little pieces and then reconstruct it into a more productive form. It is far more useful to decide on a future and then determine what kind of work is needed to get the job done.

The most forgotten platitude for leaders is that you get the kind of behavior you reward. Most companies talk collaboration, yet usually reward individual performance. Many companies are finding that bonuses and incentives tied solely to individual performances are counterproductive. Such systems reward individuals for their contribution to the process, not to the outcome or the results. Reward systems that are based on collaboration, however, are focused on results and therefore elevate the value of all productive work.

Reward collaboration; recognize individual performance. It is important to remember that you always get the type of behavior you reward—formally or informally.

The reason for creating teams to carry out missions or to complete projects is to take advantage of the power of collaboration. There are managers and workers, however, who find any kind of collective inquiry threatening. That's because most companies preach collaboration and teamwork, yet continue to base rewards on individual performance and accomplishments. In such organizations it is wiser to appear to be a one-man-show; that is, if you want to advance in the system.

Work is whatever truly needs to be done to serve the customer and the company. Meetings should be viewed as work. Meetings, however, must be useful. Education should be considered as a part of work and rewarded as such. Dreaming, thinking, planning, and acting should be honored and celebrated as a part of work.

Questions for You

1. What do I honor and celebrate as work from my employees?

2. Do my people find joy in their work?

3. Do I reward the types of behaviors I want? All the time?

4. Do I reward risk taking?

5. Do I encourage collaboration with my reward system?

6. Do my employees believe they have a stake in the company's future?

7. What percentage of my employees' time do they spend doing what they were hired to do?

8. How should our reward system be changed?

A courageous leader would call in a few courageous employees and pose each of these questions to them.

Index